THE AGE OF DATA

How Information Is Redefining Humanity

Kolade Makinde

Copyright © 2022 Kolade Makinde

All rights reserved.

No part of this book may be reproduced, distributed, or transmitted in any form or by any means, including photocopying, or other electronic or mechanical methods, without the prior written permission of the publisher, except in the case of brief quotations embodied in critical reviews and certain non-commercial uses permitted by copyright law.

TABLE OF CONTENTS

Foreword   iv
Introduction   vi

Chapter One: The Age Of Data – How Information Is Redefining Humanity   **1**

Chapter Two: The Algorithmic Society: How Ai Shapes Human Decisions.   **11**

Chapter Three: The Future Of Work: How Data Is Redefining Profession   **20**

Chapter Four: The Invisible Hand: Data-Driven Economies And Market Disruptions   **30**

Chapter Five: The Human Identity In A Hyper-Connected World   **41**

Chapter Six: Data And Democracy: The Power And Perils Of Information Control   **53**

Chapter Seven: The Ethical Dilemma: Responsibility In The Age Of Ai   **65**

Chapter Eight: The Quantum Leap: The Future Of Computing and Data Processing.   **78**

Chapter Nine: The Healthcare Revolution: Data As The Lifeline Of Medicine   **92**

Chapter Ten: The Next Frontier: Redefining Humanity Through Data   **105**

FOREWORD

We live in an age where data is no longer just a byproduct of human activity—it is the foundation upon which economies, industries, and societies are being built. Every interaction we have, every decision we make, and every technological advancement we witness is shaped by the information we generate, analyze, and leverage. The digital transformation of our world has made data the single most valuable asset of the 21st century. But with this unprecedented power comes profound questions: How do we harness data responsibly? How do we ensure that information empowers rather than exploits? And ultimately, how does the rise of data redefine what it means to be human?

This book, *The Age of Data – How Information Is Redefining Humanity*, is an exploration of the fundamental shifts brought about by the explosion of digital information. It is not just a technical deep dive into big data, artificial intelligence, and machine learning—though these are critical elements of the narrative. Rather, it is a broader reflection on the role of data in shaping economies, societies, and even our identities in ways we are only beginning to understand.

We have reached a tipping point where data is influencing not just business and technology, but governance, ethics, and even personal freedom. The decisions made today about privacy, regulation, and the ethical use of AI will determine the course of humanity's future. Whether you are a data scientist, a business leader, a policymaker, or simply someone curious about the impact of the digital revolution, this book will provide insights into the opportunities and challenges that lie ahead.

The ability to navigate, interpret, and apply data-driven insights will define success in the years to come. Those who understand and master this transformation will shape the future. This book serves as both a guide and a call to action—an invitation to critically engage with the age of data and participate in the conversation about how information is redefining humanity.

Welcome to the future.

INTRODUCTION

We are living in an era where data is no longer just a byproduct of human activity, it is the driving force behind our economies, societies, and even personal decisions. Data has transformed from static records into a dynamic and strategic asset that influences everything from business operations to healthcare, governance, and even the way we interact as individuals. In *The Age of Data – How Information Is Redefining Humanity*; we explore how the explosion of data and the rise of artificial intelligence are reshaping the fabric of our world.

Never before in human history have, we generated and consumed information at such an astonishing rate. Every second, vast amounts of data are created—through online transactions, social media interactions, IoT sensors, and artificial intelligence models. But raw data alone is not the revolution; the true transformation lies in how we harness it. With advanced algorithms, machine learning, and predictive analytics, data is now guiding billion-dollar decisions, optimizing supply chains, enabling personalized medicine, and even forecasting global events.

But with immense power comes immense responsibility. As data becomes the new currency of the digital age, ethical concerns, privacy issues, and misinformation have risen to the forefront. How do we strike a balance between innovation and responsibility? How do businesses, governments, and individuals adapt to a world where data dictates our choices? These are the pressing questions we must address as we navigate this uncharted territory.

This book will take you through the evolution of data—how it has grown from simple records to a key determinant of human progress. We will examine the industries being revolutionized, the challenges that lie ahead, and the societal shifts that come with an increasingly data-driven existence. Whether you are a data scientist, business leader, or simply someone interested in the profound changes shaping our world, *The Age of Data* will provide insights into how information is redefining humanity and what it means for our collective future.

Welcome to the age where data rules. Let's explore it together.

CHAPTER ONE

The Age of Data How Information Is Redefining Humanity

We have entered an age where data is more than just a tool. It is the foundation upon which modern society is built. From the way businesses operate to how governments make decisions and individuals interact with the world; data has become an undeniable force reshaping humanity at every level.

In today's hyper-connected world, every action generates data. Every purchase, search, social media post, and sensor reading contributes to an ocean of information, powering artificial intelligence, automation, and predictive analytics. What was once intangible—human behavior, preferences, emotions—can now be quantified, analyzed, and used to drive decisions on an unprecedented scale.

This transformation is not just about efficiency and innovation; it is fundamentally altering how we perceive ourselves and our place in the world. With real-time insights and predictive intelligence, organizations no longer rely solely on human intuition but leverage vast data ecosystems to anticipate market trends, automate complex processes and personalize experiences at a granular level.

But as data grows in influence, it also raises critical ethical and existential questions. Who controls this vast information? How do we balance privacy with progress? What happens when algorithms make decisions that affect our lives in ways we don't fully understand? The increasing role of AI and data-driven systems challenges traditional notions of responsibility, autonomy, and trust.

Moreover, the data revolution is redefining power dynamics. Countries and corporations with access to massive datasets wield an unparalleled advantage, shaping economies, policies, and even social behaviors. Meanwhile, individuals are both empowered and vulnerable, as data-driven conveniences come at the cost of surveillance and algorithmic bias.

This book delves into the profound ways in which data is reshaping industries, governance, culture, and human identity itself. It examines the promises and perils of a world driven by information, exploring how we can navigate this new reality while ensuring that data remains a force for progress rather than control.

The Age of Data is here. The question is: how will we harness its potential while safeguarding what makes us human?

The Data Revolution: A New Era of Human Advancement

The 21st century has ushered in an era where data is more valuable than oil, and information has become the foundation of progress across industries, economies, and societies. From personalized recommendations on streaming platforms to AI-driven healthcare diagnostics, data has fundamentally reshaped how we interact with technology, businesses, and even each other.

The Shift from Information Scarcity to Data Abundance

For much of human history, knowledge was scarce and difficult to disseminate. Libraries held the world's wisdom, and access to information was limited to those with privilege and power. The internet changed this dynamic, creating an ecosystem where data flows at an unprecedented scale. Every interaction, transaction, and digital footprint contributes to an ever-growing pool of information, offering insights that can drive decision-making, innovation, and societal transformation.

The Driving Forces Behind the Data Revolution

Several factors have accelerated this new era of human advancement:

Computational Power: The exponential growth in processing capabilities has made it possible to analyze vast amounts of data in real time.

AI and Machine Learning: Algorithms can now process data at scales unimaginable a few decades ago, leading to predictive analytics, automation, and intelligent decision-making.

Cloud Computing: The ability to store and access massive datasets from anywhere has democratized data usage for businesses and individuals alike.

The Internet of Things (IoT): With billions of connected devices generating continuous streams of data, real-time insights and automation are becoming a reality in industries ranging from healthcare to manufacturing.

The Impact on Industries and Society

The data revolution has not just improved efficiency, it has redefined entire industries:

Healthcare: Predictive analytics and AI-powered diagnostics are improving patient outcomes and reducing costs.

Finance: Algorithmic trading and fraud detection systems are reshaping investment strategies and risk management.

Retail and Marketing: Hyper-personalization allows businesses to tailor products and advertisements to individual consumer preferences.

Government and Policy: Data-driven governance enables smarter city planning, efficient resource allocation, and better public services.

The New Challenges of a Data-Driven World

While data has unlocked immense possibilities, it has also introduced critical challenges:

Privacy and Security: With vast amounts of personal data being collected, ethical concerns about surveillance, consent, and misuse are more pressing than ever.

Bias in AI and Data Interpretation: Algorithms are only as good as the data they are trained on. If biases exist in the data, they can perpetuate and amplify societal inequalities.

Information Overload: With so much data available, making sense of it — and ensuring its accuracy — has become a challenge in itself.

A New Paradigm for Humanity

We are at a turning point. The decisions we make today about how we collect, use, and regulate data will shape the future of human progress. The data revolution is not just about technology; it is about redefining what it means to be human in an era where information is the most powerful currency.

The Historical Shift from Knowledge to Data

Throughout history, knowledge has been the cornerstone of human progress. From ancient civilizations that relied on oral traditions and written manuscripts to the scientific revolution that introduced empirical methods, human advancement has always been driven by the accumulation and transmission of knowledge. However, we are now witnessing a fundamental shift—one where knowledge, once defined by experience and intuition, is being augmented and, in some cases, replaced by data-driven insights.

In the past, wisdom was passed down through generations, shaped by cultural narratives, human interpretation, and expert judgment. Decision-making in business, governance, and science depended largely on qualitative understanding and limited datasets. But with the rise of computing power, automation, and artificial intelligence, the paradigm has shifted. We have transitioned from relying on anecdotal evidence to harnessing vast amounts of structured and unstructured data, allowing for more precise, scalable, and predictive decision-making.

This transition has been fueled by several key technological revolutions. The emergence of the internet democratized access to information, while cloud computing enabled large-scale data storage and processing. Machine learning and AI have further accelerated the shift, transforming raw data into actionable intelligence. What was once based on human observation is now validated, optimized, and automated by algorithms capable of analyzing patterns at a scale no human mind could comprehend.

Yet, this shift is not without its complexities. The increasing reliance on data raises critical questions about trust, bias, and ethical responsibility. As we move further into an era where data informs every aspect of life—from healthcare and finance to politics and personal interactions—we must ensure that the transition from knowledge to data enhances, rather than diminishes, human understanding.

The historical shift from knowledge to data is not just a technological evolution; it is a transformation in how we perceive truth, make decisions, and shape the future of humanity. Understanding this shift is the first step in navigating *The Age of Data*.

Data as the New Currency of Power

In the digital age, power is no longer solely measured by financial wealth, military strength, or political influence. Instead, data has emerged as the most valuable resource, shaping economies, businesses, and even governments. Those who control data—whether corporations, tech giants, or nations—wield an unprecedented level of influence over markets, consumer behavior, and societal trends.

Just as oil fueled the industrial revolution, data fuels the digital revolution. Companies like Google, Amazon, and Facebook (Meta) have built trillion-dollar empires by mastering the collection, analysis, and monetization of data. From personalized recommendations to targeted advertising, they have transformed consumer insights into economic power. Governments, too, recognize the strategic importance of data—leveraging it for national security, smart cities, and artificial intelligence research that can tip the balance of global dominance.

The rise of data-driven decision-making is also reshaping traditional industries. Financial markets are now driven by algorithmic trading, manufacturing is optimized through predictive analytics, and even healthcare is seeing breakthroughs with AI-powered diagnostics. Those who can harness and interpret vast data streams gain a competitive edge, while those who fail to adapt risk obsolescence.

However, the centralization of data raises concerns about privacy, security, and ethics. The debate over data ownership, surveillance, and digital rights has become one of the most pressing issues of our time. As we move deeper into the age of data, the challenge will not just be collecting information, but ensuring it is used responsibly, equitably, and ethically.

Data is no longer just a tool — it is the new currency of power. Those who understand and master it will shape the future.

The Intersection of AI, Big Data, and Society

The convergence of artificial intelligence (AI) and big data is reshaping the very fabric of society, influencing how we work, make decisions, and interact with the world. AI-powered systems thrive on vast amounts of data, using machine learning and deep learning models to extract insights, automate processes, and enhance decision-making. As a result, the synergy between AI and big data has given rise to unprecedented capabilities in industries such as healthcare, finance, education, and governance.

At the societal level, AI-driven data analytics is transforming everything from urban planning to personalized medicine. Smart cities leverage real-time data to optimize traffic flow, reduce energy consumption, and enhance public safety. In healthcare, AI algorithms process vast amounts of patient data to predict diseases, recommend treatments, and improve medical diagnostics. Meanwhile, businesses rely on AI-driven insights to understand consumer behavior, tailor marketing strategies, and streamline supply chain operations.

However, as AI and big data integrate deeper into society, they also bring ethical dilemmas and risks. Privacy concerns have surged as companies and governments collect, store, and analyze personal data at an unprecedented scale. The potential for algorithmic bias raises questions about fairness in decision-making processes, from hiring practices to loan approvals. Moreover, the automation of tasks traditionally performed by humans raises concerns about job displacement and the future of work.

The intersection of AI, big data, and society is not just a technological revolution—it is a cultural and philosophical shift that challenges our understanding of autonomy, trust, and ethical responsibility. As we navigate this new era, striking a balance between innovation, privacy, and ethical considerations will be critical to ensuring that AI and big data serve humanity in a responsible and inclusive way.

CHAPTER TWO

The Algorithmic Society How Ai Shapes Human Decisions.

We now live in an era where algorithms play a crucial role in shaping our daily lives. From what news we read to which products we buy, artificial intelligence (AI) influences decisions both big and small—often without us realizing it. As AI systems become more sophisticated, their impact on human behavior, business strategy, and even societal values continues to grow. This chapter explores how algorithms are shaping decision-making across various domains, the ethical dilemmas they introduce, and the implications for a world increasingly driven by data.

The Invisible Hand of Algorithms

In the past, human decision-making was driven by personal experience, intuition, and available knowledge. Today, AI acts as an invisible guide, filtering information and making recommendations tailored to individual behaviors and preferences. Some key areas where algorithms have a profound influence include:

Social media and Information Consumption: Platforms like Facebook, X (formerly Twitter), and TikTok use AI to curate content feeds, amplifying engagement but also reinforcing echo chambers and influencing public opinion.

E-Commerce and Consumer Behavior: Recommendation engines on platforms like Amazon and Netflix analyze user behavior to suggest products and content, subtly shaping consumer choices.

Hiring and Workforce Decisions: AI-powered recruitment tools screen candidates, prioritizing certain qualifications and characteristics—raising concerns about bias and fairness.

Healthcare and Diagnostics: AI models assist doctors by predicting disease outcomes, influencing treatment options, and even detecting illnesses before symptoms appear.

The Ethical Dilemmas of Algorithmic Decision-Making

As algorithms take on more responsibility in shaping human choices, they introduce new ethical challenges:

Bias and Discrimination: AI models learn from historical data, which can contain societal biases. If not carefully monitored, these biases can be amplified, leading to unfair hiring practices, discriminatory lending decisions, or biased legal outcomes.

Loss of Human Agency: Over-reliance on AI can lead to diminished critical thinking and decision-making skills, as people defer to algorithmic suggestions without questioning their validity.

Transparency and Accountability: Many AI systems operate as "black boxes," making decisions that even their creators struggle to explain. This raises concerns about trust and accountability, especially in high-stakes areas like criminal justice or healthcare.

Manipulation and Misinformation: Personalized content curation can be used to manipulate opinions, spread misinformation, or exploit human psychology for profit. Deepfake technology and AI-generated propaganda add new layers of complexity to this issue.

As AI's role in decision-making continues to expand, organizations, governments, and individuals must find ways to ensure ethical and responsible AI use. Key strategies include:

Developing Explainable AI (XAI): Ensuring that AI systems provide clear, understandable reasons for their decisions can help build trust and accountability.

Algorithmic Auditing and Regulation: Governments and regulatory bodies are increasingly focused on setting guidelines for fair and transparent AI practices.

Human-AI Collaboration: Rather than replacing human judgment, AI should be seen as an augmentation tool—helping people make better decisions rather than making choices for them.

Public Awareness and Digital Literacy: Educating people about how algorithms influence their choices can help them think critically about the information they consume and the decisions they make.

A Future Driven by AI, But Controlled by Humans

The algorithmic society is not inherently good or bad—it is a reflection of the data and systems that shape it. The challenge moving forward is ensuring that AI serves humanity's best interests rather than exploiting its vulnerabilities. While AI can enhance efficiency, optimize processes, and uncover insights, it must be balanced with human judgment, ethical oversight, and a commitment to fairness.

In the coming years, the role of AI in decision-making will only deepen. How we design, regulate, and interact with these intelligent systems will determine whether they become tools for empowerment or mechanisms of control. In The Age of Data, mastering this balance is not just an opportunity, it is a necessity.

Predictive Analytics in Everyday Life

Predictive analytics, once a tool reserved for scientific research and large enterprises, has now become an integral part of everyday life. From the moment we wake up to the time we go to bed, data-driven predictions shape our decisions, experiences, and interactions—often without us even realizing it.

Every time you receive a recommendation on Netflix, Amazon, or Spotify, predictive analytics is at work, analyzing your past behavior to suggest content you're likely to enjoy. When Google Maps reroutes, your commute based on real-time traffic conditions, it's using predictive modeling to anticipate congestion before it happens. Even in healthcare, wearable devices track heart rates, activity levels, and sleep patterns, using predictive algorithms to warn users of potential health risks before symptoms manifest.

In finance, banks and credit card companies deploy predictive analytics to detect fraud, analyzing transaction patterns in real-time to identify unusual activities. E-commerce platforms leverage these insights to personalize shopping experiences, forecasting demand and optimizing supply chains to ensure products are available before customers even search for them.

Beyond consumer applications, predictive analytics is transforming industries like law enforcement, where data models anticipate crime hotspots, and in education, where student performance is analyzed to provide early intervention strategies. The power of prediction is redefining how businesses operate, how governments plan for the future, and how individuals make decisions.

While predictive analytics enhances convenience and efficiency, it also raises important ethical and privacy concerns. As algorithms make increasingly influential decisions, there is a growing need for transparency, fairness, and accountability in their application. The future of predictive analytics will not only be about improving accuracy but also ensuring that these predictions serve society in an ethical and responsible manner.

In The Age of Data, predictive analytics is more than a tool—it is a force shaping our daily lives, influencing our choices, and redefining how we engage with the world around us.

The Ethical Implications of Algorithmic Bias

As data-driven decision-making becomes deeply embedded in society, the ethical challenges surrounding algorithmic bias have become impossible to ignore. From hiring processes to loan approvals, healthcare diagnostics to law enforcement, AI-powered systems are increasingly determining outcomes that affect people's lives. However, these algorithms are only as fair as the data they are trained on—and when biases exist in that data, they can perpetuate and even amplify systemic inequalities.

Algorithmic bias can emerge in many ways. Sometimes, it stems from historical data that reflects existing societal prejudices. For example, if a hiring algorithm is trained on past employment data that favors male candidates over female ones, it may continue to discriminate, even unintentionally. Other times, bias arises from incomplete or unrepresentative datasets, leading to AI models that work well for some populations but fail for others.

This has been particularly evident in facial recognition systems, where studies have shown that accuracy rates are significantly lower for people with darker skin tones, leading to wrongful identifications and potential civil rights violations.

The consequences of unchecked algorithmic bias can be severe. In finance, biased credit scoring models may deny loans to qualified applicants from underrepresented communities. In healthcare, predictive models that are not trained on diverse patient data may misdiagnose diseases for certain demographic groups. And in the criminal justice system, biased AI-driven risk assessment tools can disproportionately label individuals from minority backgrounds as high-risk, reinforcing existing disparities in policing and sentencing.

Addressing algorithmic bias requires a multi-faceted approach. First, data collection practices must be scrutinized to ensure diversity and representativeness. Second, AI models should be regularly audited for bias, with transparent mechanisms for detecting and correcting unfair patterns. Lastly, ethical AI frameworks, government regulations, and industry standards must be enforced to hold organizations accountable for how their algorithms impact society.

As we navigate the Age of Data, ensuring that algorithms serve all of humanity fairly, not just a privileged few — is one of the greatest challenges we face. The responsibility lies not just with data scientists and engineers but with businesses, policymakers, and society as a whole.

Striking a Balance Between Automation and Human Judgment

As artificial intelligence (AI) and data-driven automation become deeply embedded in decision-making across industries, the challenge is no longer just about technological advancement — it's about ensuring that human judgment remains a critical part of the equation. While automation brings speed, efficiency, and scalability, human oversight is essential for context, ethics, and adaptability.

The Strengths of Automation

AI-powered systems can process massive datasets in real time, detecting patterns and making predictions far beyond human capability. In industries like finance, AI algorithms analyze market trends to optimize investments, while in healthcare, machine learning models assist in diagnosing diseases with greater accuracy. Automation has also revolutionized supply chains, customer service, and cybersecurity by reducing human error and increasing operational efficiency.

The Limitations of AI and the Need for Human Judgment

Despite its strengths, AI lacks emotional intelligence, moral reasoning, and the ability to navigate nuances in complex decision-making. Automated hiring tools, for instance, may reflect biases present in training data, leading to unfair outcomes. Similarly, AI-driven legal or medical decisions can miss critical contextual factors that only human professionals can interpret. These limitations highlight the need for human oversight to prevent unintended consequences.

Achieving the Right Balance

Businesses and policymakers must design frameworks where AI supports, rather than replaces, human decision-making. This means:

Human-in-the-loop Systems: Ensuring that AI-driven processes involve human intervention at key decision points, especially in high-stakes scenarios.

Ethical AI Development: Incorporating transparency, explainability, and fairness into AI models to build trust and accountability.

Continuous Learning and Adaptation Encouraging professionals to develop hybrid skills—leveraging AI while maintaining critical thinking, ethics, and domain expertise.

The future of work and decision-making will be defined not by AI replacing humans, but by a symbiotic relationship where automation enhances human capabilities rather than diminishing them. By striking this balance, we can harness the power of AI while ensuring that human judgment remains at the heart of ethical and effective decision-making.

CHAPTER THREE

The Future of Work How Data Is Redefining Profession

The nature of work is undergoing a seismic shift, driven by the rapid evolution of data and artificial intelligence. Traditional job roles are being redefined, new professions are emerging, and businesses are restructuring their operations to become more data driven. In this transformation, data is not just an enabler but a core driver of how work is done, who does it, and what skills are most valuable.

From finance to healthcare, marketing to manufacturing, data is reshaping every industry. Professionals today are expected to leverage data-driven insights for decision-making, moving away from intuition-based strategies. In finance, risk assessments and investment strategies are now built on predictive analytics rather than gut instinct. In healthcare, AI-powered diagnostics assist doctors in identifying diseases with higher accuracy. Even in creative industries, algorithms personalize content recommendations and assist in generating marketing strategies.

One of the most profound changes is the automation of routine and repetitive tasks. AI and machine learning models are taking over processes that were once labor-intensive, allowing professionals to focus on higher-value tasks like strategic thinking, innovation, and problem-solving. As a result, jobs that require human creativity, ethical judgment, and emotional intelligence are becoming more critical than ever.

However, this shift also presents challenges. The demand for data literacy is increasing across all professions. Employees who fail to upskill may find themselves struggling to stay relevant in a job market that increasingly values data fluency. Organizations, too, must rethink their workforce strategies, ensuring they balance automation with human expertise while fostering a culture of continuous learning.

Looking ahead, the future of work will not be about machines replacing humans, it will be about humans and machines working together. Companies that embrace a data-driven mindset, invest in talent development, and integrate AI responsibly will thrive in this new era. The Age of Data is not just changing what we do — it is redefining how we work, the skills we need, and the opportunities that lie ahead.

The Rise of AI-Augmented Roles

The integration of artificial intelligence into the workplace is not a distant future, it is happening now. Across industries, AI is reshaping job functions, automating routine tasks, and enhancing human capabilities in ways never before imagined.

However, instead of replacing human workers outright, AI is increasingly being used to augment their roles, enabling professionals to focus on higher-level problem-solving, creativity, and strategic decision-making.

One of the most significant shifts in AI-augmented roles is occurring in data science and analytics. AI-driven automation now handles repetitive tasks such as data cleaning, feature engineering, and even aspects of model selection. This allows data professionals to spend more time on critical thinking, ethical considerations, and interpreting complex insights that drive business strategy. Similarly, in fields like software development, AI-powered coding assistants help developers write and debug code faster, boosting productivity while allowing engineers to focus on designing innovative solutions.

Beyond technical fields, AI is also enhancing decision-making in finance, healthcare, and customer service. Financial analysts now rely on AI-driven predictive models to assess market trends, while doctors use AI-assisted diagnostics to improve patient outcomes. Customer service teams leverage AI chatbots to handle routine inquiries, freeing human representatives to resolve complex issues requiring empathy and nuanced understanding.

However, the rise of AI-augmented roles also raises critical questions about the skills professionals need to thrive in this evolving landscape. While technical literacy remains essential, the most valuable skills of the future will be those that AI cannot easily replicate—creativity, emotional intelligence, adaptability, and ethical reasoning. The ability to work alongside AI, leveraging its strengths while compensating for its limitations, will define success in the modern workforce.

Organizations must also take responsibility for ensuring that AI augmentation enhances human potential rather than diminishing job opportunities. Investing in workforce training, upskilling programs, and ethical AI deployment will be key to achieving a balance where AI serves as a collaborative tool rather than a disruptive force.

In the Age of Data, AI-augmented roles represent both an opportunity and a challenge. Those who embrace this transformation—developing new skills and adapting to AI-driven workflows—will be well-positioned to thrive in a world where human and machine intelligence work in tandem to drive progress.

Data Science as a Core Business Function

Data science is no longer a niche discipline reserved for tech companies and research institutions—it has become a fundamental driver of business success across industries. Organizations that treat data as a strategic asset rather than a byproduct of operations gain a significant competitive advantage, enabling smarter decision-making, enhanced customer experiences, and increased efficiency.

From Support Function to Strategic Priority

Traditionally, data analytics was seen as a support function, used mainly for reporting and basic trend analysis. However, in the modern business landscape, data science is deeply integrated into core operations. Companies now leverage predictive analytics, machine learning, and AI-driven insights to optimize everything from marketing campaigns to supply chain logistics and risk management.

Data-Driven Decision-Making at Scale

Executives increasingly rely on data science to guide strategic decisions. Whether it's forecasting market trends, identifying operational bottlenecks, or personalizing customer interactions, data science helps businesses move beyond intuition to make evidence-based choices. By embedding data-driven insights into everyday decision-making processes, companies enhance agility and responsiveness in a rapidly evolving market.

Building a Data-Centric Culture

For data science to function as a core business asset, organizations must foster a culture where data literacy is widespread. This means:

Empowering employees with data tools and training to make informed decisions.

Ensuring cross-functional collaboration between data teams and business units to align insights with strategic goals.

Implementing strong data governance to maintain data quality, security, and compliance.

The Competitive Edge of Data-Driven Enterprises

Leading companies such as Amazon, Google, and Tesla have demonstrated how deeply integrated data science can drive innovation. From AI-powered product recommendations to autonomous vehicle technology, these businesses exemplify how leveraging data science as a core function leads to sustained growth and disruption in their industries.

For businesses that want to thrive in the Age of Data, treating data science as a fundamental part of operations—rather than a secondary support role—is no longer optional. Those that fail to embrace this shift risk falling behind in an increasingly data-driven world.

Upskilling in the Age of Machine Learning

As machine learning and artificial intelligence (AI) reshape industries, the demand for new skills is accelerating. The traditional career paths of data professionals, engineers, and business leaders are evolving, requiring continuous learning and adaptation. In **The Age of Data**, upskilling is no longer optional—it is essential for survival in a rapidly changing digital economy. This chapter explores why upskilling is critical, which skills are in high demand, and how individuals and organizations can stay ahead in the machine learning era.

Why Upskilling Matters in the Age of AI

Machine learning is automating routine tasks, augmenting decision-making, and transforming entire professions. However, rather than replacing jobs outright, AI is shifting the skill sets required to remain competitive. The key drivers for upskilling include:

The Rise of Automation: AI-powered tools automate data processing, analytics, and even coding tasks. Professionals must move beyond repetitive tasks and focus on high-level problem-solving.

Demand for AI Fluency: Businesses increasingly expect employees — not just data scientists — to understand how AI and machine learning influence decision-making. Basic AI literacy is becoming a core competency across industries.

Interdisciplinary Skills Are Key: The most valuable professionals today are those who can bridge technical expertise with business acumen, ethics, and communication skills.

Lifelong Learning is the New Normal: In a field evolving as rapidly as machine learning, degrees and certifications can quickly become outdated. The ability to learn and adapt continuously is more valuable than any single qualification.

Key Skills for the Machine Learning Era

Upskilling in the age of machine learning requires a combination of technical, analytical, and soft skills. The most in-demand skills include:

Data Literacy and Statistical Thinking: Understanding how data is collected, processed, and analyzed is crucial for anyone working with AI-driven tools.

Machine Learning Fundamentals: While not everyone needs to be an AI engineer, professionals should grasp core ML concepts such as supervised learning, unsupervised learning, and deep learning.

Cloud Computing and Big Data Technologies: Platforms like AWS, Google Cloud, and Microsoft Azure are critical for deploying scalable AI solutions.

Ethics and Responsible AI: As AI systems make more decisions, professionals must understand algorithmic bias, fairness, and explainability to ensure ethical AI implementation.

Communication and Data Storytelling: The ability to translate complex insights into actionable business decisions is a highly valuable skill in any industry.

Strategies for Effective Upskilling

Both individuals and organizations must take proactive steps to stay ahead of AI-driven transformations. Key strategies include:

Self-Learning and Online Courses: Platforms like Coursera, edX, and Udacity offer specialized courses in AI, data science, and machine learning.

Hands-on Projects and Hackathons: Practical experience is crucial for mastering machine learning concepts. Participating in competitions on Kaggle or real-world projects can accelerate learning.

On-the-Job Training and AI Mentorships: Companies should foster continuous learning through internal AI training programs and mentorship initiatives.

Cross-Disciplinary Learning: Professionals should explore fields outside of their core expertise — such as psychology, business strategy, or design — to enhance their ability to work in AI-driven environments.

Company-Wide AI Adoption Programs: Businesses must invest in AI education across all levels, ensuring that teams can leverage machine learning effectively.

Thriving in the Age of Data

The era of machine learning is not just about automation; it is about augmentation. AI will enhance human capabilities rather than replace them, but only for those willing to adapt. Upskilling is the key to unlocking opportunities in this data-driven world. Whether you're a data scientist, business leader, or entrepreneur, continuous learning will determine your success in **The Age of Data**.

CHAPTER FOUR

The Invisible Hand Data-Driven Economies and Market Disruptions

Data has become the new currency of the global economy, driving unprecedented market shifts and reshaping traditional economic structures. Much like Adam Smith's "invisible hand" guided free markets through supply and demand, today's economies are increasingly steered by data — an invisible force optimizing efficiency, predicting consumer behavior, and redefining competitive advantages.

In the past, industries relied on historical trends and human intuition to make business decisions. Now, real-time data analytics, machine learning, and AI models empower companies to predict demand, automate supply chains, and personalize customer experiences with precision. Retailers use predictive analytics to optimize inventory levels, financial institutions leverage AI to detect fraud in milliseconds, and digital platforms refine algorithms to maximize user engagement and revenue.

This data-driven economy has also disrupted traditional market leaders. Companies that fail to adapt to this new paradigm risk obsolescence. Brick-and-mortar retail giants have been overtaken by e-commerce platforms powered by big data. Legacy media companies struggle against streaming services that use analytics to curate content. Even the financial sector is being transformed by fintech startups utilizing AI-driven investment strategies.

However, the rise of data-driven economies presents challenges. Market monopolization by tech giants raises concerns about fair competition, privacy, and ethical data usage. Countries are grappling with regulatory policies to ensure transparency and prevent misuse of consumer data. The digital divide is also widening, as businesses with robust data infrastructures gain a significant advantage over those struggling to adapt.

Despite these challenges, the invisible hand of data is here to stay. Organizations that harness their power responsibly will gain agility, efficiency, and deeper customer insights. As data continues to redefine economies and disrupt markets, businesses must embrace change, invest in data-driven strategies, and navigate the evolving digital landscape with foresight and adaptability.

The Business Models of the Digital Age

The rise of data as a strategic asset has fundamentally reshaped how businesses operate, compete, and generate value. Traditional revenue models are being disrupted, and organizations that successfully adapt to the data-driven economy are gaining unprecedented competitive advantages. In the digital age, businesses are no longer just selling products or services — they are monetizing data, leveraging AI-driven insights, and creating new ecosystems fueled by information.

1. Data as a Product and Service

In today's economy, data itself has become a valuable commodity. Companies like Google, Meta, and Amazon have built trillion-dollar empires by collecting, analyzing, and monetizing user data. Many businesses now offer "data-as-a-service" (DaaS), where insights derived from analytics, consumer behavior, and predictive modeling are sold to other organizations. This model allows companies to unlock new revenue streams by providing access to unique datasets, industry trends, or AI-powered decision-making tools.

2. The Subscription and Platform Economy

The subscription-based model has become a dominant force in the digital age, allowing companies to generate consistent revenue while building long-term customer relationships. From software-as-a-service (SaaS) companies like Microsoft and Salesforce to media platforms like Netflix and Spotify, the shift to recurring payments has redefined business sustainability. Many of these platforms utilize AI-driven personalization, data analytics, and user insights to continuously enhance customer experience, ensuring higher engagement and retention.

Another powerful model is the platform-based economy, where businesses create ecosystems that connect users, sellers, and service providers. Companies like Uber, Airbnb, and Alibaba thrive by acting as intermediaries, leveraging data to optimize transactions, match supply and demand, and enhance user experiences. These platforms continuously evolve through machine learning algorithms that analyze user behavior, pricing trends, and logistics.

3. AI-Driven Automation and Efficiency

Businesses are increasingly integrating AI-driven automation to streamline operations, reduce costs, and scale efficiently. Predictive analytics, process automation, and intelligent decision-making systems help companies optimize supply chains, marketing strategies, and workforce management. AI-powered customer service bots, personalized marketing algorithms, and automated fraud detection systems are now standard tools for digital enterprises, enabling them to deliver more efficient and personalized services.

4. The Rise of Decentralized and Blockchain-Based Models

As concerns about data privacy, security, and centralization grow, new business models leveraging blockchain and decentralized systems are emerging. Decentralized finance (DeFi), non-fungible tokens (NFTs), and decentralized autonomous organizations (DAOs) are transforming industries by enabling peer-to-peer transactions, smart contracts, and token-based economies. Companies exploring these models aim to remove intermediaries, enhance transparency, and empower users with greater control over their digital assets.

Adapting to the Digital Economy

For businesses to thrive in the Age of Data, embracing these new models is not optional, it's essential. Companies must rethink how they leverage data, invest in AI-driven capabilities, and align their business strategies with emerging technological trends. The future belongs to those who can harness data not just as a resource but as a core driver of innovation, decision-making, and value creation.

Data Monetization and the Ownership Dilemma

In the Age of Data, information was not just a byproduct of business operations, it was a valuable commodity. Companies across industries are finding ways to extract financial value from data, turning it into a revenue-generating asset through insights, targeted advertising, and even direct sales. However, with this transformation comes a critical question: who truly owns the data, and how should it be used responsibly?

The Rise of Data as a Revenue Stream

Enterprises today generate vast amounts of data from customer interactions, operational processes, and IoT devices. This data holds immense potential for:

- Enhanced decision-making through predictive analytics.

- Personalized marketing via targeted recommendations.

- Selling insights to third-party businesses.

- Creating new business models, such as data-driven financial services and AI-powered automation.

Tech giants like Google, Meta, and Amazon have built entire ecosystems around data monetization, refining algorithms that maximize ad revenue, product recommendations, and even dynamic pricing. However, as more companies seek to capitalize on data, the ethical and legal implications grow more complex.

Who Owns the Data?

Ownership of data is a growing point of contention. Key stakeholders include:

- Consumers, who generate data through their online and offline activities.

- Businesses, which collect, process, and analyze data to extract value.

- Governments, which regulate how data is stored, shared, and monetized.

With increasing awareness of privacy rights, customers are demanding more control over their personal information. Regulations like the GDPR (General Data Protection Regulation) in Europe and CCPA (California Consumer Privacy Act) in the

U.S. are reshaping the way companies handle data ownership and consent.

Balancing Profitability with Ethics

The challenge lies in leveraging data for business growth while ensuring transparency, consumer trust, and regulatory compliance. Companies must navigate:

Consent and transparency: Clearly communicating how data is collected and used.

Data security: Preventing breaches and unauthorized access.

Fair value exchange: Ensuring consumers benefit from their data contributions, such as through personalized experiences or financial incentives.

The Future of Data Monetization

As AI and machine learning continue to evolve, data monetization strategies will become even more sophisticated. The rise of decentralized data ownership models, powered by blockchain and Web3, could give users more control over their data and enable direct monetization. Meanwhile, businesses that adopt privacy-first approaches — such as differential privacy and federated learning — will be better positioned to build long-term consumer trust.

Ultimately, the companies that strike the right balance between profitability, ethics, and regulatory compliance will lead the data economy of the future.

The Role of Privacy and Cybersecurity in Economic Stability

In an era where data drives economies, the intersection of privacy, cybersecurity, and economic stability has never been more critical. As businesses, governments, and individuals generate and rely on vast amounts of digital information, ensuring its security is fundamental to maintaining trust, financial resilience, and sustainable economic growth. This chapter explores the profound impact of data privacy and cybersecurity on economic stability, the risks of failing to protect digital assets, and strategies for building a secure data-driven future.

The Economic Consequences of Data Breaches

Cyberattacks are no longer isolated incidents — they are systemic risks capable of disrupting industries and entire economies. Some of the most significant economic consequences of data breaches include:

Financial Losses and Business Disruptions: Ransomware attacks, intellectual property theft, and fraud can cost companies billions in direct financial losses and operational downtime. The 2017 WannaCry attack, for example, caused an estimated $4 billion in damages worldwide.

Loss of Consumer Trust: When companies mishandle personal data, customers lose confidence. The 2018 Facebook-Cambridge Analytica scandal led to a decline in user engagement and regulatory scrutiny, impacting Facebook's market value.

Regulatory Fines and Legal Repercussions: Governments are tightening data protection laws, with regulations such as GDPR (General Data Protection Regulation) and CCPA (California Consumer Privacy Act) imposing hefty fines for non-compliance. In 2021, Amazon was fined $887 million for GDPR violations, highlighting the financial risks of poor data governance.

National Security and Economic Espionage: Cyberattacks targeting critical infrastructure, financial systems, or intellectual property threaten national economies. State-sponsored attacks have become a key geopolitical concern, with nations investing heavily in cybersecurity to protect their competitive advantages.

Privacy as an Economic Asset

Data privacy is no longer just a compliance requirement — it is an economic differentiator. Companies that prioritize consumer privacy can gain competitive advantages, including:

Customer Loyalty and Brand Strength: Organizations that demonstrate a commitment to data privacy build stronger relationships with customers, leading to increased retention and long-term growth. Apple, for example, has positioned itself as a leader in consumer privacy, enhancing its brand reputation.

Innovation and Ethical AI Development: Privacy-focused businesses encourage responsible AI adoption, ensuring that data-driven technologies are developed with transparency and fairness in mind.

Cross-Border Trade and Global Compliance: Companies that adhere to strict privacy standards can operate seamlessly across international markets, avoiding legal conflicts and fostering trust with foreign partners.

Cybersecurity as a Pillar of Economic Stability

Cybersecurity is not just about protecting data, it is about ensuring business continuity, financial market stability, and national security. Key components of a strong cybersecurity framework include:

Zero-Trust Architecture: Organizations are moving away from traditional perimeter-based security models and adopting a zero-trust approach, where every access request is verified.

AI-Powered Threat Detection: Machine learning algorithms are enhancing cybersecurity by detecting anomalies and identifying threats in real time.

Collaboration Between Public and Private Sectors: Governments and businesses must work together to combat cyber threats, sharing intelligence and developing unified security policies.

Resilience Planning and Incident Response: Companies that implement proactive risk management strategies can minimize financial losses and recover faster from cyber incidents.

Building a Secure and Stable Data Economy

The future of economic stability depends on how well societies manage the delicate balance between data innovation and security. Governments, enterprises, and individuals must take collective action by:

Strengthening Global Data Protection Laws: Ensuring that regulations evolve with technological advancements while fostering a standardized approach to data privacy.

Investing in Cybersecurity Talent: Addressing the global shortage of cybersecurity professionals by prioritizing workforce development and education.

Enhancing Digital Literacy: Empowering individuals to protect their personal data and recognize cybersecurity threats in their daily interactions.

As we navigate the **Age of Data**, privacy and cybersecurity are no longer just technical concerns—they are economic imperatives. Organizations that fail to adapt will face increasing financial and reputational risks, while those that embrace security and privacy will be the foundation of a resilient, trustworthy digital economy.

CHAPTER FIVE

The Human Identity in a Hyper-Connected World

The explosion of data in the digital age has not only transformed industries and economies but also reshaped our very sense of identity. In a world where every action, preference, and interaction generates a digital footprint, the boundaries between the physical and virtual selves are becoming increasingly blurred. Our identities are no longer just shaped by personal experiences and social interactions—they are also defined by algorithms, data-driven recommendations, and digital profiles curated by technology.

From social media platforms to biometric recognition systems, data now dictates how individuals are perceived, how opportunities are granted, and how relationships are formed. Personalized content feeds shape opinions, predictive hiring models influence career prospects, and AI-driven health diagnostics provide insights into personal well-being. This hyper-connected environment creates both empowerment and vulnerability: while data offers convenience and tailored experiences, it also raises concerns about privacy, autonomy, and digital bias.

Moreover, the digitalization of identity has deep ethical implications. Who controls our data? How do we ensure that digital identities remain an extension of personal autonomy rather than a tool for manipulation? Governments and organizations are increasingly grappling with questions of data ownership, digital rights, and the ethical use of AI in identity verification and decision-making.

As we move deeper into the age of data, the challenge lies in balancing hyper-connectivity with personal agency. To maintain authenticity in an era of algorithmic influence, individuals must become more data-literate, organizations must prioritize ethical AI practices, and societies must establish frameworks that protect digital identities while fostering innovation. The future of human identity will be shaped by our ability to harness data responsibly while preserving the fundamental values of privacy, individuality, and human dignity.

The Digital Footprint: How Data Shapes Personal Identity

In an era where nearly every action leaves a trace, our digital footprint has become an extension of our identity. From social media interactions to online purchases, biometric data, and even passive location tracking, the information we generate forms a digital profile that reflects who we are—sometimes more accurately than we realize. The Age of Data has redefined personal identity, raising critical questions about privacy, ownership, and the influence of algorithms on our lives.

1. The Data We Leave Behind

Every online interaction contributes to a growing repository of personal data. Websites track browsing habits through cookies, social media platforms analyze engagement patterns, and smart devices collect behavioral insights. Even offline activities — such as using credit cards, visiting locations with GPS-enabled smartphones, or interacting with IoT-connected devices — leave behind digital markers that can be aggregated and analyzed.

This data is not just stored; it is actively used to shape user experiences. Algorithms determine what content we see, what ads we receive, and even which financial or healthcare options are available to us. As a result, our digital footprint becomes more than just a record of past activity — it actively influences future interactions and opportunities.

2. Data Ownership and Control

One of the most pressing debates in the digital age is the question of who truly owns personal data. While individuals generate data through their interactions, corporations, governments, and third-party entities often have more control over it. Tech giants collect vast amounts of personal information, often without explicit consent or full transparency about how it will be used.

With the rise of data privacy regulations like GDPR (General Data Protection Regulation) and CCPA (California Consumer Privacy Act), there is increasing pressure on organizations to return control of data to users. However, challenges remain in implementing meaningful consent mechanisms, ensuring secure data storage, and providing individuals with the ability to manage or delete their digital footprints.

3. Algorithmic Identity and Perception

Beyond raw data collection, algorithms analyze and categorize individuals based on patterns of behavior, preferences, and even inferred traits. AI-driven profiling can impact everything from job opportunities to credit scores and medical diagnoses. This has led to concerns about algorithmic bias—where automated decisions reinforce stereotypes or exclude certain groups based on flawed or incomplete data.

Social media platforms, for example, curate content feed using machine learning algorithms that prioritize engagement. While this enhances user experience, it also creates "filter bubbles" that reinforce existing beliefs, shaping personal identity based on limited or biased information. Similarly, facial recognition technology, which is becoming increasingly widespread, raises ethical concerns about surveillance, identity theft, and false identifications.

4. Redefining Identity in the Digital Age

As digital footprints grow more complex, the concept of identity is evolving. People are no longer defined solely by their physical presence or traditional identifiers like names and addresses. Instead, they exist across multiple digital profiles — some created by themselves, others constructed by algorithms, data brokers, or government databases.

To navigate this new landscape, individuals and businesses must take an active role in managing digital identities. This includes adopting privacy-focused tools, advocating for ethical data policies, and understanding how AI-driven systems impact personal and professional opportunities. The balance between convenience and privacy, transparency and control, will ultimately shape how identity is perceived and protected in the Age of Data.

The Psychological Effects of Data-Driven Personalization

In today's digital landscape, data-driven personalization has become an integral part of how individuals interact with technology. From curated content on streaming platforms to hyper-targeted advertisements and AI-driven recommendations, businesses leverage vast amounts of data to create customized experiences. While this personalization enhances user engagement and convenience, it also carries significant psychological implications, some beneficial, others deeply concerning.

The Comfort of Personalization: A Tailored Experience

- At its best, personalization makes users feel understood. Algorithms that analyze past behaviors, preferences, and interactions help deliver:

- More relevant content, reducing the time spent searching for information or entertainment.

- A sense of familiarity, reinforcing user preferences through customized feeds.

- Improved efficiency, with automation streamlining decision-making, such as smart assistants predicting needs before they arise.

For many, this leads to increased satisfaction, reduced decision fatigue, and a more seamless digital experience. Businesses, in turn, benefit from greater engagement, higher retention rates, and increased sales.

The Echo Chamber Effect: Reinforcing Biases

One of the unintended consequences of hyper-personalization is the reinforcement of existing beliefs and preferences. Algorithms prioritize content that aligns with a user's past interactions, often at the cost of exposure to diverse perspectives. This results in:

- Filter bubbles, where users are only exposed to viewpoints that confirm their opinions.

- Polarization, particularly in areas like politics, social issues, and news consumption.

- Reduced critical thinking, as individuals are less likely to encounter challenging or opposing viewpoints.

In extreme cases, this can lead to misinformation, radicalization, or a skewed perception of reality, as users become trapped in digital environments that reflect and reinforce their biases.

Privacy Concerns and the Feeling of Being Watched

While personalization enhances convenience, it also raises significant concerns about privacy and surveillance. Many users report feeling uneasy about:

- The extent to which companies track their behaviors, from browsing history to location data.

- Targeted ads that feel intrusive, sometimes appearing seconds after a conversation or search.

- The loss of autonomy, as algorithms dictate choices without users fully realizing it.

Psychologically, this can create feelings of discomfort, distrust, and anxiety about digital interactions. The growing awareness of data privacy issues has led to increasing demand for transparency and user control over personal data.

Balancing Personalization with Autonomy

As data-driven personalization continues to evolve, businesses must balance engagement with ethical responsibility. Key strategies include:

- Transparent data usage policies, ensuring users understand how their information is collected and applied.

- User-controlled personalization settings, allowing individuals to adjust their experience.

- Ethical AI and responsible recommendation algorithms, designed to prioritize well-being over engagement metrics.

Ultimately, while data-driven personalization has the power to enhance user experiences, it must be implemented with careful consideration of its psychological effects. The future of personalized technology should empower users, not manipulate them, ensuring that convenience and choice remain in their hands.

Privacy vs. Convenience: Where Do We Draw the Line?

The digital world offers unprecedented convenience. With just a few taps on a smartphone, we can access financial services, receive personalized recommendations, and navigate cities in real time. However, this ease of access comes at a cost—our personal data. As businesses and governments increasingly collect, analyze, and monetize user information, society faces a critical question: Where do we draw the line between privacy and convenience?

The Trade-Off: What Are We Willing to Sacrifice?

The modern digital experience thrives on data. Algorithms personalize content, AI streamlines decision-making, and businesses optimize services based on behavioral insights. But every convenience we enjoy often involves sharing personal data, whether knowingly or unknowingly.

Personalized Services vs. Data Exposure: Streaming platforms, e-commerce sites, and social media personalized recommendations based on past interactions. While this improves user experience, it also creates detailed digital profiles that can be exploited.

Seamless Transactions vs. Surveillance: Contactless payments, smart assistants, and digital IDs enhance convenience but also raise concerns about who has access to sensitive financial and biometric data.

AI Assistants vs. Always-On Listening: Virtual assistants like Siri, Alexa, and Google Assistant improve efficiency but require constant data collection, leading to concerns over surveillance and data breaches.

The Business of Data: Who Controls It?

Data is often referred to as the "new oil"—a valuable asset that fuels economic growth and technological innovation. However, the centralization of data among a few tech giants has created power imbalances.

Big Tech and the Data Economy: Companies like Google, Facebook, and Amazon build their business models around collecting and monetizing user data, often under opaque terms of service.

Government Surveillance and National Security: Governments argue that collecting data enhances security, prevents crime, and improves public services. However, mass surveillance programs, such as China's social credit system or past revelations from the NSA, raise ethical concerns.

Decentralized Data Ownership: Emerging technologies like blockchain and self-sovereign identity systems aim to give users greater control over their data, reducing dependency on centralized platforms.

The Public Perception of Privacy

Surveys show a paradox: while people express concern over privacy, many willingly trade their data for convenience. This phenomenon, known as the **"privacy paradox,"** highlights the complexity of digital trust.

Generational Differences: Younger generations, who grew up in a connected world, often prioritize convenience over privacy. Older generations tend to be more cautious about data sharing.

Crisis Moments and Changing Attitudes: Data scandals like the Cambridge Analytica breach or major ransomware attacks temporarily heighten public awareness, but behavioral changes are often short-lived.

Regulatory Responses: Governments worldwide are introducing stricter data protection laws, such as GDPR in Europe and CCPA in California, to empower consumers with greater transparency and control.

Finding the Balance: Can We Have Both?

The future of digital privacy hinges **on finding the right balance**—preserving convenience without compromising individual rights. Possible solutions include:

Privacy-First Design: Companies can adopt privacy-enhancing technologies (PETs), such as encryption, anonymization, and differential privacy, to ensure user data remains protected.

User Empowerment: Giving individuals more control over their data, through opt-in models and transparent consent mechanisms, can help rebuild trust.

Stronger Regulations: Governments must enforce policies that hold companies accountable for data misuse while promoting innovation-friendly regulations.

Digital Literacy: Educating users about privacy risks and how to protect their data can help them make more informed choices.

As we navigate the Age of Data, the tension between privacy and convenience will continue to shape the way we interact with technology. The key challenge is not just drawing a line—it's about redesigning the digital ecosystem to prioritize ethical, secure, and user-centric experiences.

CHAPTER SIX

Data And Democracy the Power and Perils of Information Control

In the digital age, data has become one of the most influential forces shaping democracy. Information flows faster than ever before, enabling unprecedented levels of political engagement, activism, and transparency. At the same time, the power to control, manipulate, or restrict data has raised critical concerns about misinformation, privacy, and the very foundations of democratic governance.

On one hand, data has strengthened democratic participation. Citizens now have access to vast amounts of information, real-time updates, and direct channels of communication with policymakers. Data-driven governance enables governments to make informed decisions, predict societal trends, and implement policies that reflect real-world needs. Digital platforms empower individuals, fostering civic engagement and holding institutions accountable.

On the other hand, the power of data can also be exploited, threatening the principles of free and fair democracy. The spread of misinformation, deep-fake technology, and algorithmic bias has made it easier than ever to manipulate public opinion. Targeted political advertising, powered by massive datasets, can reinforce echo chambers, creating polarized societies where individuals are exposed only to information that aligns with their existing beliefs. Additionally, the increasing surveillance capabilities of both governments and corporations pose serious ethical concerns about privacy, freedom of speech, and the potential misuse of personal data.

The balance between data-driven governance and individual rights is one of the defining challenges of modern democracy. Nations must establish clear regulatory frameworks that protect against data exploitation while ensuring that information remains accessible and transparent. The role of artificial intelligence in governance, electoral processes, and policymaking must be carefully managed to prevent bias and uphold democratic integrity.

As we navigate the complexities of data and democracy, the future will depend on our ability to create systems that leverage information for collective progress while safeguarding against its potential for harm. Ensuring that data remains a tool for empowerment, rather than control, will be key to preserving democratic values in the age of information.

The Influence of Data on Political Narratives

In the Age of Data, politics was no longer just about speeches, debates, and policies is deeply intertwined with data-driven strategies that shape public opinion and influence electoral outcomes. From targeted digital campaigns to algorithmically amplified misinformation, the role of data in modern politics has transformed how narratives are constructed, disseminated, and received.

1. Microtargeting and Personalized Political Messaging

Political campaigns have long relied on data to understand voter behavior, but with the rise of big data and AI-driven analytics, microtargeting has reached unprecedented levels. Campaigns collect vast amounts of voter data—from social media activity and browsing history to purchasing behavior and geolocation—to create highly personalized messages tailored to specific demographics.

For example, data-driven political advertising allows campaigns to segment voters based on factors like age, education, ideology, and even personality traits. A swing voter in a suburban district may receive different messaging than a young urban progressive, even if they are watching the same platform. While this approach can increase engagement, it also raises concerns about manipulation, as voters are shown selective information that reinforces their existing beliefs.

2. Social Media, Bots, and the Spread of Misinformation

Social media has become a dominant battleground for political discourse, with platforms like Twitter, Facebook, and TikTok influencing millions of voters worldwide. However, the use of data-driven algorithms to promote engagement has also led to the spread of misinformation, propaganda, and polarizing content.

Automated boats and troll farms, often powered by AI, amplify false narratives at scale, making it difficult for users to distinguish between organic and artificial discourse. The viral nature of misinformation means that once a false claim spreads, it can be nearly impossible to contain, even after being debunked. In many cases, political actors exploit this phenomenon to shape public perception, undermine opponents, or create confusion around key issues.

3. The Rise of Data-Driven Political Polarization

One of the unintended consequences of data-driven politics is the increasing polarization of societies. Social media algorithms prioritize engagement, often by showing users content that aligns with their preferences and biases. This creates "filter bubbles" and echo chambers, where individuals are exposed primarily to viewpoints that reinforce their existing beliefs.

As a result, political discourse becomes more divisive, with less room for nuanced discussion or compromise. The ability of data analytics to hyper-personalize political content means that individuals may be receiving completely different versions of reality based on their data profiles. This raises critical questions about democracy, informed decision-making, and the role of digital platforms in shaping public opinion.

4. Ethical Considerations and the Future of Data in Politics

The intersection of data and politics presents significant ethical challenges. The use of voter data without consent, algorithmic biases that favor certain narratives, and the weaponization of misinformation all pose risks to democratic integrity. In response, governments and regulatory bodies are increasingly pushing for transparency in political advertising, stricter data privacy laws, and AI accountability frameworks.

At the same time, data can be a force for good in politics. Open data initiatives, fact-checking AI tools, and blockchain-based voting systems have the potential to increase transparency, combat disinformation, and restore trust in democratic processes. The challenge for the future will be finding a balance between leveraging data for political engagement while ensuring ethical standards and protecting democratic values.

The Weaponization of Misinformation and Deepfakes

In the Age of Data, information was more powerful than ever — but it is also more vulnerable to manipulation. The rise of misinformation and deepfakes has fundamentally altered how people perceive reality, trust media, and engage with the world.

While data has the potential to drive progress, it can just as easily be weaponized to mislead, influence, and destabilize societies.

The Rise of Misinformation in a Data-Driven World

Misinformation, the spread of false or misleading content—has existed for centuries, but today's digital landscape has amplified its reach and impact. With social media algorithms prioritizing engagement over accuracy, falsehoods can spread faster than the truth. The key drivers of misinformation include:

- Algorithmic amplification, where sensational or emotionally charged content gets prioritized.

- Echo chambers, where individuals are exposed only to information that reinforces their beliefs.

- AI-generated content, which allows false narratives to be mass-produced with increasing sophistication.

From political propaganda to health misinformation, the consequences can be severe, shaping public opinion and even influencing global events.

Deepfakes: The Next Frontier of Digital Deception

Deepfakes—AI-generated media that manipulates video and audio to create hyper-realistic but false content—represent a new and dangerous evolution of misinformation. With advances in machine learning, deepfakes are becoming increasingly difficult to detect. Their applications range from entertainment and satire to more malicious uses, such as:

Impersonation scams, where deepfake technology is used to mimic voices and deceive individuals or businesses.

Political manipulation, where falsified videos of public figures can sway elections or ignite unrest.

Corporate sabotage, with fake statements from executives affecting stock markets or reputations.

As deepfakes become more sophisticated, they undermine trust in all forms of media, making it harder to distinguish truth from fiction.

The Psychological and Societal Impact

The widespread presence of misinformation and deepfakes has profound effects on individuals and societies:

- Erosion of trust, as people become skeptical of all sources, including legitimate ones.

- Polarization, where manipulated content deepens divisions and fuels conflict.

- Decision paralysis, as uncertainty makes it harder to distinguish reliable information.

In extreme cases, misinformation campaigns can influence elections, destabilize economies, and even incite violence. The ability to control narratives through data manipulation has become a powerful tool for bad actors, from cybercriminals to nation-states.

Fighting Back: The Role of Data Science and AI

While AI has contributed to the problem, it is also part of the solution. Efforts to combat misinformation and deepfakes include:

- AI-driven detection tools, which analyze content for signs of manipulation.

- Blockchain for content verification, ensuring the authenticity of digital media.

- Fact-checking initiatives, using machine learning to verify claims in real time.

- Media literacy programs, empowering individuals to critically assess information.

Governments, tech companies, and researchers must work together to create policies and technologies that mitigate the spread of misinformation. In an era where data is both a weapon and a shield, safeguarding truth is one of the greatest challenges of our time.

Can Data-Driven Governance Enhance Democracy?

In the digital age, data has become a fundamental tool for decision-making, governance, and policy formulation. Governments now have access to vast amounts of data that can be leveraged to improve public services, enhance transparency, and make informed policy decisions. However, while data-driven governance holds the potential to strengthen democracy, it also presents significant ethical, privacy, and bias-related challenges.

The Promise of Data-Driven Governance

The idea behind data-driven governance is simple: by using advanced analytics, artificial intelligence, and real-time data streams, governments can operate more efficiently, predict societal trends, and create policies that better reflect the needs of their citizens. Some key advantages include:

Enhanced Public Services: Cities use data to optimize transportation, healthcare, and energy consumption, improving overall quality of life. Smart city initiatives, like Singapore's data-driven urban planning, help reduce congestion, pollution, and inefficiencies.

Informed Policy Decisions: Governments can analyze economic indicators, employment trends, and social behaviors to craft policies based on real-world evidence rather than assumptions.

Transparency and Accountability: Open data initiatives allow citizens to access government records, budgets, and decisions, reducing corruption and increasing trust in public institutions.

Predictive Governance: AI-powered models can help anticipate crises, from pandemics to financial downturns, allowing for proactive responses rather than reactive measures.

The Risks and Challenges

Despite these benefits, data-driven governance comes with significant risks that could undermine democracy rather than enhance it.

Bias and Discrimination: If data is biased or incomplete, AI-driven policies may reinforce existing inequalities. Predictive policing algorithms, for example, have been criticized for disproportionately targeting marginalized communities.

Mass Surveillance and Privacy Violations: Governments collecting extensive data on citizens can lead to intrusive surveillance, eroding civil liberties. China's social credit system is an example of data-driven governance being used for control rather than empowerment.

Manipulation and Misinformation: Data can be weaponized to influence public opinion, as seen in cases where AI-powered disinformation campaigns have affected elections and policy debates.

Lack of Public Understanding and Consent: Many citizens are unaware of how their data is being used in governance, raising concerns about informed consent and ethical data practices.

Striking the Right Balance

For data-driven governance to truly enhance democracy, it must be implemented with safeguards that ensure fairness, transparency, and accountability. Key strategies include:

Ethical AI Frameworks: Governments must establish strict guidelines to prevent bias and misuse of AI in policy decisions.

Privacy-First Policies: Data collection should be limited to what is necessary, with clear protections against misuse.

Citizen Involvement: Governments should encourage participatory decision-making, where citizens have a say in how data is used for governance.

Regulatory Oversight: Independent agencies should oversee data-driven policies to prevent abuse and ensure ethical implementation.

When applied responsibly, data-driven governance has the power to make democracy more responsive, efficient, and inclusive. However, without proper checks and balances, it could just as easily become a tool for control and discrimination. The challenge is not whether to use data in governance, but how to ensure that its use aligns with the fundamental principles of democracy — transparency, fairness, and citizen empowerment.

CHAPTER SEVEN

The Ethical Dilemma Responsibility in the Age of Ai

As artificial intelligence continues to shape industries, economies, and daily life, the question of ethical responsibility has never been more urgent. Who is accountable when an AI system makes a harmful decision? How do we ensure that AI remains a tool for progress rather than a force of unintended consequences? The rise of AI presents both incredible opportunities and profound ethical dilemmas that society must address.

AI systems are increasingly making decisions that impact human lives—from medical diagnoses and financial approvals to hiring processes and criminal justice. While these technologies can improve efficiency and accuracy, they also introduce biases, privacy risks, and a loss of human oversight. Many AI models are trained on historical data that may reflect societal inequalities, leading to decisions that reinforce discrimination rather than eliminate it. Without careful regulation and transparency, AI can become a mechanism for deepening social divides rather than bridging them.

One of the biggest challenges is balancing innovation with responsibility. Companies and governments are racing to develop AI-driven solutions, but ethical considerations often lag behind technological advancements. Should AI be allowed to make life-or-death decisions in healthcare? How do we prevent autonomous systems from being weaponized? These are not just technical questions, they are moral ones that require collaboration between technologists, policymakers, ethicists, and the public.

Another pressing concern is accountability. When AI systems fail, who is to blame? If an autonomous vehicle causes an accident or a biased algorithm denies someone a loan, should the responsibility lie with the developers, the company deploying the system, or the regulators overseeing it? Establishing clear ethical frameworks and legal standards for AI accountability is essential to prevent harm and build trust in these technologies.

The future of AI ethics depends on proactive measures rather than reactive solutions. Organizations must prioritize fairness, transparency, and inclusivity in AI development. Governments must establish policies that protect individuals from AI-driven discrimination and ensure that AI applications align with human values. Most importantly, society must recognize that ethical AI is not just about preventing harm—it is about creating a future where technology enhances human well-being rather than undermining it.

The Bias Problem in AI Models

Artificial intelligence has become a cornerstone of modern decision-making, powering applications in finance, healthcare, hiring, law enforcement, and more. However, a growing concern within the AI community is the issue of bias embedded within these models. AI is often perceived as neutral, but in reality, it inherits the biases present in the data it is trained on. This bias problem has significant implications for fairness, ethics, and the role of AI in shaping society.

1. How Bias Creeps into AI Models

Bias in AI is not the result of intentional programming; rather, it emerges through several factors:

Training Data Bias: AI models learn from historical data, which may contain patterns of discrimination. For example, if an AI system is trained in hiring records that reflect historical gender disparities, it may continue to favor certain demographics over others.

Sampling Bias: When the dataset does not adequately represent the diversity of the population, the AI model may make inaccurate or unfair predictions. This is particularly problematic in facial recognition systems, where models trained predominantly on lighter-skinned individuals perform poorly on darker-skinned faces.

Algorithmic Bias: Certain machine learning algorithms may inadvertently amplify existing biases. Reinforcement learning models, for instance, optimize for efficiency rather than fairness, potentially reinforcing societal inequalities.

Human Bias in AI Development: Developers and data scientists, often unknowingly, introduce their own biases into AI models through decisions about feature selection, model tuning, and evaluation metrics.

2. Real-World Consequences of AI Bias

The consequences of biased AI extend beyond technical concerns—they impact people's lives in profound ways:

Discriminatory Hiring Algorithms: Some AI-powered recruitment tools have been found to disadvantage women and minority candidates due to biased training data.

Unfair Credit and Loan Decisions: AI models used in finance sometimes deny loans or set higher interest rates for certain racial or socioeconomic groups.

Biased Criminal Justice Systems: Predictive policing algorithms have disproportionately targeted minority communities, reinforcing systemic biases in law enforcement.

Healthcare Disparities: AI-driven diagnostic tools may be less accurate for underrepresented populations, leading to unequal medical outcomes.

3. Strategies to Mitigate AI Bias

Addressing AI bias requires a multi-faceted approach that combines technical, regulatory, and ethical interventions:

Bias Audits and Fairness Testing: Organizations must conduct regular audits to detect and mitigate bias in their AI models. Tools like IBM's AI Fairness 360 and Google's What-If Tool help identify disparities in model predictions.

Diverse and Representative Data: Expanding training datasets to include a broader representation of demographics can help reduce bias. This includes actively collecting data from underrepresented groups.

Algorithmic Transparency and Explainability: AI systems should be designed to provide clear explanations for their decisions. Explainable AI (XAI) techniques help identify and correct biased decision-making.

Regulatory and Ethical Guidelines: Governments and institutions are introducing AI ethics frameworks to enforce fairness. The EU's AI Act, for example, seeks to regulate high-risk AI applications to prevent discrimination.

4. The Future of Fair AI

As AI becomes more deeply integrated into society, ensuring fairness and accountability is no longer optional, it is a necessity. The future of AI will depend on continuous improvements in data governance, ethical AI development, and interdisciplinary collaboration between technologists, policymakers, and social scientists. While bias may never be completely eliminated, proactive efforts can help minimize its impact, making AI a tool for progress rather than perpetuating existing inequalities.

Who Owns Data? Legal and Moral Perspectives

As data becomes the most valuable asset of the digital era, a critical question emerges: Who truly owns it? Is it the individuals who generate it, the companies that collect it, or the governments that regulate it? The answer is complex, intertwining legal, ethical, and societal dimensions. In *The Age of Data*, ownership is not just about possession — it's about control, accountability, and the power to shape the future.

The Legal Landscape: A Battle for Data Ownership

Legally, data ownership is a contested space with no universal framework. Different jurisdictions interpret ownership in distinct ways:

- Personal Data Protection Laws – Regulations like the General Data Protection Regulation (GDPR) in the EU and the California Consumer Privacy Act (CCPA) in the U.S. grant individuals some control over their personal data but stop short of full ownership rights.

- Corporate Data Control – Many businesses argue that once users interact with their platforms, the data generated belongs to the company, enabling them to monetize it through analytics, advertising, and AI training.

- Government Oversight – Some nations claim authority over citizens' data for national security or public interest reasons, leading to concerns about surveillance and privacy breaches.

The absence of clear, global data ownership laws creates uncertainty and often leaves individuals with limited say in how their data is used.

The Moral Dilemma: Rights vs. Profits

Beyond legal debates, data ownership raises deep ethical concerns. Companies harvest vast amounts of personal information, often without the users' full understanding or explicit consent. This leads to several moral questions:

- Do individuals have the right to monetize their own data, just as corporations do?

- Should companies be required to share profits generated from user data with the people who created it?

- At what point does data collection become an invasion of privacy rather than a fair exchange for services?

Moral perspectives differ widely. Some argue that personal data is an extension of the individual and should be treated as personal property. Others believe that once data is shared with a service provider, it becomes a mutual asset with shared responsibilities.

Big Tech, Data Brokers, and the Business of Information

A handful of technology giants control an overwhelming portion of the world's data. Platforms like Google, Facebook, and Amazon process immense datasets, fueling AI models, targeted advertising, and predictive analytics. In parallel, data brokers — companies that collect, aggregate, and sell consumer data — operate largely in the shadows, creating extensive profiles on individuals without their direct involvement.

This raises concerns about:

- Transparency – Many users are unaware of how much of their data is being tracked, stored, and sold.

- Consent – Opting out of data collection is often difficult, with vague policies and complex settings discouraging users from taking control.

- Ethical Use – The potential for discrimination, manipulation, and exploitation grows as data is weaponized for profit and influence.

The Future: Towards a Fairer Data Economy

As awareness of data ownership grows, there are increasing calls for reform. Potential solutions include:

- Data as Personal Property – Granting individuals full ownership of their data, allowing them to sell or license it as they see fit.

- Decentralized Data Markets – Using blockchain and Web3 technologies to enable individuals to control and monetize their data independently.

- Stronger Regulation – Governments enforcing stricter rules on data collection, usage, and monetization to protect consumers.

The question of data ownership is far from settled. As societies grapple with the consequences of an information-driven world, striking a balance between innovation, privacy, and ethical responsibility will define the future of digital civilization.

Ensuring Transparency and Accountability in AI Systems

As artificial intelligence (AI) continues to influence decision-making across industries, ensuring transparency and accountability has become a critical concern. AI systems are now responsible for making decisions in healthcare, finance, hiring, policing, and governance—areas where errors or biases can have severe consequences. Without clear mechanisms for oversight, these systems risk becoming black boxes, where decisions are made without human understanding or accountability.

Why Transparency Matters

Transparency in AI refers to the ability of humans to understand how AI models arrive at their decisions. This is essential for several reasons:

Trust and Adoption: Users are more likely to trust AI systems when they understand how they function and why they make certain recommendations.

Bias Detection and Fairness: A transparent system allows researchers and regulators to identify biases and correct them before they cause harm.

Regulatory Compliance: Many industries require explainability for legal and ethical reasons, such as GDPR's right to explanation for automated decisions.

Improved Model Performance: When AI models are transparent, developers can debug and refine them more effectively.

Challenges in Achieving AI Transparency

Despite its importance, AI transparency remains a challenge due to:

Complexity of AI Models: Deep learning algorithms often operate in ways that are difficult to interpret, even by their creators.

Trade-Off Between Accuracy and Explainability: Many highly accurate models, such as neural networks, are less interpretable than simpler models like decision trees.

Corporate Secrecy: Some organizations hesitate to disclose their AI decision-making processes due to intellectual property concerns.

Lack of Standardized Metrics: There is no universal framework for measuring AI transparency, making it difficult to assess and compare different systems.

Ensuring Accountability in AI

Accountability ensures that when AI systems make harmful or biased decisions, there are mechanisms in place to correct and prevent future occurrences. Strategies for ensuring accountability include:

Regulatory Oversight: Governments and industry bodies should enforce AI governance policies to hold companies responsible for biased or unfair AI decisions.

Explainable AI (XAI): Developing AI models that provide clear, understandable reasoning behind their outputs can improve accountability.

Human-in-the-Loop Systems: Keeping humans involved in AI decision-making processes can help mitigate risks and ensure fairness.

Auditability and Monitoring: Regular audits of AI systems can help identify and address biases, security flaws, or unintended consequences.

Ethical AI Guidelines: Companies should adopt ethical AI principles, such as Google's AI ethics framework or the EU's guidelines on trustworthy AI.

Balancing Innovation with Responsible AI

While ensuring transparency and accountability is crucial, organizations must also balance these principles with innovation and efficiency. Striking this balance involves:

Developing Interpretable AI Without Sacrificing Performance: Using hybrid approaches that combine explainable models with powerful deep learning techniques.

Creating AI Ethics Committees: Establishing internal review boards that oversee AI deployments and address ethical concerns.

Public Engagement and Education: Making AI transparency a societal conversation rather than just a technical one, ensuring citizens understand and have a say in AI policies.

As AI continues to shape the modern world, ensuring its transparency and accountability is not just a technical necessity but a societal imperative. The future of AI must be one where its benefits are widely accessible, its risks are mitigated, and its decision-making processes are clear and fair for all.

CHAPTER EIGHT

The Quantum Leap the Future of Computing and Data Processing

As we approach the limits of classical computing; a new frontier is emerging—one that promises to redefine how we process and analyze data. Quantum computing, once a theoretical concept, is rapidly becoming a reality, with the potential to revolutionize industries, scientific research, and artificial intelligence. But what does this quantum leap mean for the future of data science, security, and computation?

Quantum computing differs fundamentally from classical computing. While traditional computers process information using bits (0s and 1s), quantum computers use qubits, which can exist in multiple states simultaneously thanks to the principles of superposition and entanglement. This enables quantum computers to perform complex calculations exponentially faster than today's most powerful supercomputers, unlocking new possibilities in cryptography, optimization, and machine learning.

One of the most immediate impacts of quantum computing will be on data security. Many of today's encryption methods, which protect everything from financial transactions to personal communications, rely on the difficulty of factoring large numbers—a task that classical computers struggle with. Quantum computers, however, could break these encryptions in seconds, forcing organizations to rethink cybersecurity strategies and develop quantum-resistant cryptographic methods.

Beyond security, quantum computing has the potential to transform data-driven fields such as pharmaceuticals, climate modeling, and artificial intelligence. For example, quantum simulations could lead to breakthroughs in drug discovery by modeling molecular interactions at an unprecedented scale. In AI, quantum computing could accelerate the training of machine learning models, allowing for deeper insights and more sophisticated pattern recognition.

However, the quantum revolution is still in its early stages. Practical, large-scale quantum computers are years—if not decades—away from widespread adoption. The field faces challenges such as qubit stability, error correction, and the development of quantum algorithms that can outperform classical methods in real-world applications. Nevertheless, the race is on, with tech giants and research institutions making significant strides toward unlocking quantum computing's full potential.

As quantum technology matures, businesses and data professionals must prepare for its implications. Organizations will need to develop strategies for integrating quantum computing into their operations, while also safeguarding against the disruptive changes it may bring. The transition from classical to quantum computing will not happen overnight, but those who stay ahead of the curve will be best positioned to harness the power of this new era of computation.

The Advent of Quantum Computing and AI

As the world moves further into the age of data, quantum computing is emerging as a revolutionary force with the potential to redefine artificial intelligence. Traditional computing, built on binary logic, reaches the limits of its capabilities in processing complex data on a scale. Quantum computing, leveraging the principles of quantum mechanics, offers exponential processing power that could transform AI development, optimization, and decision-making. This chapter explores how quantum computing is poised to reshape AI, the challenges ahead, and the profound implications for data science and beyond.

1. How Quantum Computing Enhances AI

Quantum computing differs from classical computing in several keyways:

Superposition: Unlike traditional bits, which are either 0 or 1, quantum bits (qubits) can exist in multiple states simultaneously. This allows quantum computers to perform vast numbers of calculations in parallel, accelerating AI training and inference.

Entanglement: Qubits can be entangled, meaning the state of one qubit is directly related to another, regardless of distance. This property can enhance AI's ability to process interconnected datasets more efficiently.

Quantum Parallelism: Classical AI models rely on iterative processing, but quantum algorithms can explore multiple solutions at once, enabling faster optimization and more advanced machine learning capabilities.

By leveraging these principles, quantum AI has the potential to solve problems that are currently intractable for even the most powerful supercomputers.

2. Transforming AI Through Quantum Computing

Quantum computing promises breakthroughs in several AI-related fields:

Optimization Problems: Many AI applications, from logistics to financial modeling, require solving complex optimization problems. Quantum algorithms like Grover's and QAOA (Quantum Approximate Optimization Algorithm) vastly improve efficiency in these domains.

Drug Discovery and Materials Science: AI models for molecular simulations demand immense computational power. Quantum computing can accelerate these simulations, leading to faster discoveries in medicine and materials engineering.

Natural Language Processing (NLP): Quantum-enhanced NLP models could process language patterns at an unprecedented scale, improving machine translation, sentiment analysis, and contextual understanding.

Cryptography and Security: Quantum computing poses both risks and solutions for AI-driven cybersecurity. While quantum algorithms can break traditional encryption, they also pave the way for quantum-resistant cryptographic methods.

3. Challenges of Quantum AI Adoption

Despite its promise, quantum computing faces several hurdles:

Hardware Limitations: Quantum computers require highly controlled environments with extreme cooling conditions. Current quantum processors are still in their early stages, limiting widespread adoption.

Error Rates and Stability: Qubits are highly susceptible to noise and decoherence, leading to errors in computations. Developing error-correction techniques is a major area of research.

Integration with Existing AI Systems: Most AI models are built for classical architectures. Creating hybrid quantum-classical models that leverage the strengths of both will be crucial for practical implementation.

Skill Gaps and Accessibility: Quantum computing requires specialized expertise, and there is currently a shortage of professionals trained in both quantum mechanics and AI. Bridging this gap will be essential for progress.

4. The Future of AI in the Quantum Era

As quantum hardware matures, we can expect to see transformative shifts in AI capabilities:

Hybrid AI Models: The future will likely involve AI systems that integrate quantum and classical computing, leveraging quantum power for specific tasks while maintaining compatibility with existing infrastructure.

New Paradigms in Machine Learning: Quantum-enhanced machine learning models could redefine pattern recognition, reinforcement learning, and generative AI, leading to breakthroughs across industries.

Democratization of Quantum Computing: Cloud-based quantum computing services from companies like IBM, Google, and D-Wave are already making quantum resources available to researchers and enterprises, accelerating adoption.

While still in its infancy, the convergence of quantum computing and AI represents one of the most exciting frontiers in technology. As these advancements unfold, they will redefine what is possible in data science, automation, and intelligent decision-making, ushering in a new era of computational power.

Edge Computing and the Evolution of Data Storage

As data generation skyrockets, traditional centralized storage models are being pushed to their limits. The rise of edge computing is transforming how, where, and when data is processed, moving it closer to its source and reducing reliance on massive cloud-based infrastructures. This shift is redefining the efficiency, speed, and security of data-driven systems, impacting industries from healthcare and finance to smart cities and autonomous vehicles.

The Limits of Centralized Cloud Storage

For years, cloud computing has been the backbone of modern data infrastructure, offering scalability and accessibility. However, as real-time processing becomes critical, traditional cloud storage faces several challenges:

- Latency Issues – Transmitting data to and from centralized cloud servers can create delays, which is unacceptable for applications like autonomous driving or industrial automation.

- Bandwidth Constraints – The exponential growth of IoT devices and sensor networks places enormous strain on network bandwidth.

- Security Risks – Centralized data storage creates single points of failure, making systems vulnerable to breaches and cyberattacks.

These challenges have paved the way for a decentralized approach—edge computing.

What is Edge Computing?

Edge computing moves data processing and storage closer to the data source rather than relying on remote cloud servers. This approach reduces latency, improves efficiency, and enhances privacy by keeping sensitive data local.

Key characteristics of edge computing include:

- Localized Processing – Data is analyzed on edge devices such as IoT sensors, smartphones, or autonomous machines, minimizing the need for cloud transmission.

- Faster Decision-Making – Real-time insights are generated instantly, enabling applications like predictive maintenance and automated trading.

- Reduced Cloud Dependency – While cloud storage remains essential for long-term data retention, edge computing reduces the need for continuous data transfer.

How Edge Computing is Transforming Data Storage

The evolution of data storage is shifting towards a hybrid model where cloud and edge infrastructures work together. This transformation is evident in:

- Federated Data Architectures – Companies are adopting decentralized storage systems that distribute workloads across multiple locations.

- AI at the Edge – Machine learning models are being deployed on edge devices to enable local decision-making without sending data to centralized servers.

- Security and Compliance Enhancements – Sensitive data can be processed locally, reducing exposure to potential breaches and simplifying regulatory compliance.

The Future of Edge Computing in Data Science

As edge computing continues to evolve, we can expect:

- Smarter IoT Networks – Billions of devices operating autonomously with minimal cloud dependence.

- Energy-Efficient AI – Low-power AI models running on edge devices, making real-time analytics more sustainable.

- New Business Models – Decentralized computing creating opportunities for industries to optimize operations and reduce costs.

Edge computing represents a fundamental shift in how data is processed and stored, making information more accessible, secure, and efficient in an increasingly digital world. Businesses that embrace this evolution will gain a competitive edge in the Age of Data.

How Emerging Technologies Will Redefine Data Analytics

The field of data analytics is undergoing a radical transformation driven by emerging technologies. Traditional analytics focused on descriptive and diagnostic insights—what happened and why. However, advancements in artificial intelligence (AI), quantum computing, and edge computing are pushing data analytics into a new era, enabling predictive and prescriptive capabilities that redefine how businesses, governments, and individuals interact with data.

AI and Machine Learning: Automating Intelligence

Artificial intelligence and machine learning (ML) have fundamentally changed data analytics by automating complex pattern recognition and decision-making. Key developments include:

Automated Data Preparation: AI-driven tools now handle tedious tasks like data cleaning, anomaly detection, and feature engineering, reducing human intervention.

Predictive Analytics at Scale: Traditional analytics focused on historical data, but ML models can now forecast future trends with remarkable accuracy, allowing organizations to make proactive decisions.

Natural Language Processing (NLP): Advanced NLP enables AI systems to analyze unstructured text data, extracting meaningful insights from documents, social media, and customer interactions.

These advancements make data analytics more efficient, reducing the need for manual intervention and allowing professionals to focus on strategy rather than data wrangling.

Quantum Computing: Unlocking New Analytical Possibilities

Quantum computing has the potential to revolutionize data analytics by solving problems that are currently computationally infeasible. While still in its early stages, its implications for data analytics include:

Faster Optimization Algorithms: Quantum computing can process massive datasets exponentially faster, enabling real-time analytics on an unprecedented scale.

Enhanced Encryption and Security: The ability to break classical encryption methods forces the development of quantum-resistant security protocols, making data analytics more secure.

Complex Simulations: Industries such as pharmaceuticals, finance, and logistics can use quantum simulations to model intricate scenarios that traditional computing cannot handle efficiently.

Although quantum computing is not yet mainstream, businesses investing in quantum-ready analytics will gain a competitive edge in the coming years.

Edge Computing and Real-Time Analytics

With the rise of the Internet of Things (IoT), edge computing is reshaping data analytics by enabling real-time processing at the source of data generation. Key benefits include:

Lower Latency: Data is processed closer to its origin, reducing the time needed to derive insights and act on them.

Bandwidth Efficiency: Rather than transmitting massive amounts of raw data to centralized cloud servers, only relevant, processed insights are sent, improving efficiency.

Privacy and Security: Sensitive data remains on local devices rather than being transferred over networks, enhancing data security and compliance with privacy regulations.

This shift towards edge analytics allows businesses to make faster, data-driven decisions, particularly in industries like autonomous vehicles, manufacturing, and smart cities.

Blockchain for Data Integrity and Trust

Blockchain technology is emerging as a powerful tool for enhancing data integrity and transparency in analytics. By leveraging decentralized ledgers, organizations can:

Ensure Data Authenticity: Immutable records prevent unauthorized alterations, making data more reliable.

Enhance Auditability: Transactions and changes in datasets can be tracked with full transparency, improving accountability.

Enable Secure Data Sharing: Smart contracts facilitate secure, controlled access to datasets across organizations without exposing sensitive information.

As businesses increasingly rely on data for decision-making, blockchain can provide the trust layer necessary for analytics in finance, healthcare, and supply chain management.

The Future of Data Analytics

The convergence of these emerging technologies — AI, quantum computing, edge computing, and blockchain — will redefine how organizations extract value from data. The future of analytics will be:

More Automated: AI-driven tools will reduce human intervention, making analytics more efficient and scalable.

More Secure and Transparent: Blockchain and encryption technologies will ensure data integrity and regulatory compliance.

More Real-Time: Edge computing will enable instantaneous insights, transforming industries that rely on fast decision-making.

More Predictive and Prescriptive: Advanced modeling techniques will shift analytics from reactive reporting to proactive strategy formulation.

As we enter the age of data, organizations that embrace these innovations will gain a significant advantage, unlocking new opportunities for growth, efficiency, and competitive differentiation.

CHAPTER NINE

The Healthcare Revolution Data as The Lifeline of Medicine

In the modern age, data is not just transforming industries, it is saving lives. The healthcare sector is undergoing a profound shift, where data-driven insights are reshaping everything from diagnostics to treatment, drug discovery, and patient care. With the rise of electronic health records (EHRs), wearable devices, and AI-powered analytics, healthcare is evolving into a more precise, predictive, and personalized field.

Medical data has become one of the most valuable assets in the world. Hospitals, research institutions, and pharmaceutical companies rely on vast datasets to identify disease patterns, improve treatment protocols, and accelerate drug development. For example, predictive analytics can help detect early signs of chronic diseases, enabling preventive measures before conditions become severe. Similarly, AI-driven imaging technologies can analyze radiology scans with higher accuracy than human radiologists, leading to faster and more reliable diagnoses.

The COVID-19 pandemic demonstrated the power of data in healthcare on a global scale. Governments and medical researchers used real-time data to track the spread of the virus, predict infection rates, and allocate medical resources effectively. Vaccine development, which traditionally takes years, was accelerated through data-driven simulations and genomic sequencing, highlighting how information can drive medical breakthroughs.

Wearable health technology is another game-changer. Devices such as smartwatches and continuous glucose monitors generate real-time health data, allowing individuals to track their well-being and enabling doctors to make data-informed decisions remotely. This shift towards personalized medicine means that treatments can be tailored to an individual's genetic profile, lifestyle, and environmental factors, making healthcare more effective and less invasive.

However, with great power comes great responsibility. The increasing reliance on medical data raises significant ethical and privacy concerns. Patient data security, regulatory compliance, and the risk of algorithmic biases in AI-driven healthcare solutions must be carefully managed. Organizations must strike a balance between leveraging data for innovation and safeguarding patient confidentiality.

As data continues to redefine medicine, the future of healthcare will be built on the foundation of advanced analytics, AI-driven decision-making, and real-time monitoring. The ability to harness this data responsibly will determine how effectively we combat diseases, improve quality of life, and ultimately extend human longevity in the age of information.

Precision Medicine and AI-Driven Diagnoses

The fusion of artificial intelligence (AI) with precision medicine is transforming the healthcare landscape, ushering in a new era of data-driven, personalized treatments. Instead of the traditional one-size-fits-all approach, AI-powered precision medicine tailors' medical decisions, treatments, and interventions to the individual characteristics of each patient, leveraging vast amounts of genetic, environmental, and lifestyle data. This chapter explores how AI is revolutionizing diagnostics, optimizing treatment plans, and enhancing patient outcomes through predictive analytics and machine learning models.

1. AI's Role in Precision Medicine

Precision medicine relies on identifying patterns in complex biological and medical data to make targeted healthcare decisions. AI enhances this process in several ways:

Genomic Analysis: AI models analyze vast genetic datasets to identify mutations linked to diseases, helping in early detection and risk assessment for conditions such as cancer, Alzheimer's, and rare genetic disorders.

Predictive Analytics: Machine learning algorithms can predict a patient's likelihood of developing specific conditions based on medical history, genetics, and lifestyle factors, enabling proactive intervention.

Personalized Drug Response: AI can assess how individual patients metabolize drugs, optimizing dosages and reducing adverse effects, leading to more effective treatment plans.

Biomarker Discovery: AI helps identify biomarkers — biological indicators of disease — allowing for more precise targeting of therapies in conditions like cancer and autoimmune diseases.

2. AI-Driven Diagnostics: Speed and Accuracy

Medical diagnostics have historically relied on physician expertise and traditional imaging techniques. AI is now accelerating and enhancing this process with remarkable accuracy:

Medical Imaging and Radiology: AI-powered image recognition tools analyze X-rays, MRIs, and CT scans, detecting anomalies such as tumors, fractures, and neurological disorders with high precision.

Pathology and Histology: AI-driven models examine tissue samples to detect cancerous cells, reducing human error and speeding up diagnosis.

Wearable and Remote Monitoring: AI-enabled devices collect real-time health data, flagging irregularities in heart rate, glucose levels, and other vital to enable early intervention.

3. Challenges in AI-Driven Precision Medicine

Despite its transformative potential, AI in precision medicine faces several challenges:

Data Privacy and Security: Patient data is highly sensitive, and ensuring compliance with regulations like HIPAA and GDPR is critical. Robust security measures are required to protect against breaches and misuse.

Bias and Fairness in AI Models: AI algorithms trained on biased datasets can lead to disparities in diagnosis and treatment recommendations. Addressing these biases is essential to ensure equitable healthcare outcomes.

Integration with Healthcare Systems: Many hospitals and clinics still use legacy systems, making the integration of AI-driven tools complex and expensive. Bridging this gap requires significant investment in infrastructure.

Ethical Considerations: AI-driven decision-making in medicine raises ethical concerns, such as accountability in case of misdiagnoses and the potential reduction of human oversight in critical medical decisions.

4. The Future of AI in Precision Medicine

As AI technology advances, precision medicine will continue to evolve in several key areas:

AI-Powered Drug Discovery: Pharmaceutical companies are using AI to identify new drug candidates, reducing development time and costs.

Real-Time AI Diagnostics: Point-of-care AI systems will allow for instant diagnosis, improving accessibility to medical care, especially in remote areas.

AI and Robotics in Surgery: AI-assisted robotic surgery is enhancing precision and reducing recovery times, leading to better patient outcomes.

Digital Twin Technology: AI-driven simulations of an individual's biological systems will allow doctors to test treatment plans virtually before applying them in real life.

By harnessing AI in precision medicine, healthcare is becoming more targeted, efficient, and patient-centric. As technology continues to advance, we move closer to a future where medical care is not just reactive but proactive, predicting and preventing diseases before they take hold.

Real-Time Health Monitoring and Predictive Analytics

The healthcare industry is undergoing a transformative shift as real-time health monitoring and predictive analytics become integral to patient care. The convergence of wearable technology, IoT sensors, and AI-driven data processing is enabling unprecedented levels of personalized medicine, early disease detection, and operational efficiency. This evolution is not only improving patient outcomes but also reshaping the entire healthcare ecosystem.

From Reactive to Proactive Healthcare

Traditionally, healthcare has been reactive. Patients seek medical attention after symptoms appear. However, real-time health monitoring is shifting the paradigm to proactive and preventive care. With the proliferation of smart devices, continuous health tracking is becoming the norm, allowing for early intervention before a condition escalates.

Wearables such as smartwatches, fitness trackers, and biosensors now collect vast amounts of data, including:

- Heart rate variability
- Blood oxygen levels (SpO2)
- Glucose levels for diabetics
- ECG readings for arrhythmia detection

- Sleep patterns and stress indicators

This real-time data empowers individuals to take control of their health while giving medical professionals deeper insights into patient well-being.

The Role of Predictive Analytics in Healthcare

Predictive analytics leverages AI and machine learning to analyze vast datasets and forecast potential health risks. By identifying patterns and correlations, predictive models can:

- Detect early signs of diseases such as diabetes, heart disease, and cancer

- Predict hospital readmissions, reducing strain on healthcare systems

- Optimize treatment plans based on real-time patient responses

- Assist in personalized drug recommendations and dosage adjustments

Hospitals and healthcare providers are increasingly using AI-driven models to streamline operations, manage patient care more effectively, and reduce unnecessary medical procedures.

Challenges in Implementing Real-Time Health Monitoring

While the benefits of real-time health monitoring and predictive analytics are immense, several challenges must be addressed:

- Data Privacy and Security – Health data is highly sensitive, and ensuring compliance with regulations like HIPAA and GDPR is critical.

- Interoperability – Many healthcare systems still rely on legacy infrastructure that struggles to integrate with modern IoT devices and AI-driven platforms.

- Data Overload – Managing and making sense of continuous real-time health data requires robust AI models and efficient processing capabilities.

The Future of Data-Driven Healthcare

Looking ahead, the integration of AI, edge computing, and 5G technology will further enhance real-time health monitoring. We can expect:

- More Advanced Wearables – Devices capable of real-time blood diagnostics and early detection of neurological disorders.

- Personalized Treatment Plans – AI-driven analysis will tailor treatments to individual genetic profiles and lifestyle factors.

- AI-Assisted Telemedicine – Predictive analytics will enable virtual consultations to be more data-driven and proactive.

As healthcare moves into the Age of Data, the ability to leverage real-time monitoring and predictive analytics will be essential in creating a more efficient, effective, and patient-centered system.

The Ethics of Data Sharing in Healthcare

In the age of data-driven medicine, healthcare organizations, researchers, and policymakers face a critical challenge: balancing the benefits of data sharing with ethical concerns related to privacy, security, and informed consent. The ability to exchange patient information across institutions and geographies has led to groundbreaking advancements in personalized medicine, predictive analytics, and pandemic response. However, it also raises concerns about data ownership, potential misuse, and the rights of individuals.

Balancing Innovation with Patient Privacy

Healthcare data is among the most sensitive forms of personal information. While sharing data can accelerate medical discoveries, improve diagnostics, and enhance patient outcomes, it also introduces risks:

Privacy Violations: Unauthorized access to medical records can lead to discrimination, stigma, and financial harm for patients.

Re-identification Risks: Even anonymized data can sometimes be re-identified by cross-referencing with other datasets, putting patient confidentiality at risk.

Lack of Informed Consent: Patients often do not fully understand how their data is used, raising ethical questions about transparency and autonomy.

Regulatory Frameworks and Ethical Standards

To address these ethical concerns, governments and healthcare institutions have implemented regulations such as HIPAA (Health Insurance Portability and Accountability Act) in the U.S. and GDPR (General Data Protection Regulation) in Europe. These laws aim to:

- Establish strict data protection measures.

- Ensure that patients provide informed consent for data usage.

- Hold organizations accountable for data breaches and misuse.

However, ethical challenges persist, particularly in cross-border data sharing and the use of AI in healthcare. Standardizing global data governance policies is crucial to maintaining trust and protecting patient rights.

The Role of AI and Big Data in Healthcare Ethics

AI-driven analytics and machine learning have the potential to revolutionize healthcare, from early disease detection to precision medicine. But with this power comes responsibility. Ethical concerns include:

Bias in AI Models: If training datasets lack diversity, AI algorithms can reinforce healthcare disparities.

Data Ownership: Should patients have control over their own medical data? Or do healthcare providers and research institutions hold that right?

Commercialization of Health Data: The sale of anonymized medical records raises concerns about the commodification of patient information.

A Path Forward: Ethical Data Sharing in Healthcare

For healthcare to fully harness the power of data while maintaining ethical integrity, organizations must adopt transparent, patient-centered data practices. This includes:

- Implementing decentralized, privacy-preserving technologies such as federated learning.

- Giving patients more control over their data, including opt-in and opt-out mechanisms.

- Encouraging collaboration between policymakers, technologists, and medical professionals to create ethical guidelines for AI and data usage.

Ultimately, ethical data sharing in healthcare requires a delicate balance between innovation and individual rights. By prioritizing transparency, fairness, and patient consent, the industry can unlock the full potential of data-driven medicine without compromising trust or privacy.

CHAPTER TEN

The Next Frontier Redefining Humanity Through Data

As we enter the Age of Data, the way we live, work, and interact is undergoing a profound transformation. From artificial intelligence shaping decision-making to the ethical dilemmas of data ownership, humanity is standing at the precipice of a new era. The integration of data-driven technologies into every aspect of society presents both unprecedented opportunities and formidable challenges. The question is no longer just about how we use data — but how data is redefining what it means to be human.

A Hyper-Connected World

The exponential growth of data, fueled by IoT devices, edge computing, and cloud infrastructure, has created a hyper-connected world where every action, preference, and decision generates valuable insights. This connectivity enables seamless experiences — automated homes that anticipate our needs, intelligent cities that optimize traffic flow, and personalized healthcare that adapts to our biological rhythms. But with this interconnectivity comes concerns over surveillance, autonomy, and digital dependency.

The Rise of AI-Augmented Humanity

Artificial intelligence is no longer a futuristic concept, it is embedded in our daily lives, from recommendation engines to autonomous systems. The next frontier involves AI not just assisting but enhancing human capabilities. Neural interfaces, brain-computer interactions, and AI-driven creativity challenge traditional notions of intelligence and individuality. Will we evolve into a species where human cognition and artificial intelligence merge? If so, what does that mean for identity, decision-making, and free will?

The Data Economy and Digital Inequality

Data is the new currency, but access to it is not evenly distributed. Tech giants hold vast repositories of information, creating a digital power imbalance. As nations race to regulate and monetize data, new economic models are emerging. Who controls the data? How can businesses and individuals claim ownership of their digital footprints? Addressing these questions will be critical in ensuring that the benefits of the data revolution are shared rather than concentrated.

Ethics, Autonomy, and the Future of Decision-Making

As AI systems take on more responsibility — managing investments, diagnosing illnesses, even influencing elections — the ethics of algorithmic decision-making become increasingly complex. Bias, transparency, and accountability remain pressing concerns. The challenge ahead is not just technological but philosophical: How do we ensure that data-driven decisions align with human values?

The Human Role in a Data-Driven Future

Despite automation, predictive analytics, and AI advancements, one thing remains clear—human adaptability is irreplaceable. The next frontier is not just about what data can do, but how we, as a society, choose to navigate this transformation. Will we use data to build a more inclusive, efficient, and ethical world? Or will we allow it to widen existing divides and erode personal freedoms? The choices we make today will define the future of humanity in the Age of Data.

How Data Will Reshape Human Creativity and Innovation

For centuries, creativity and innovation have been seen as uniquely human abilities—fueled by intuition, imagination, and experience. However, in the age of data, the landscape of creativity is undergoing a fundamental transformation. With the rise of artificial intelligence, machine learning, and vast data-driven insights, human ingenuity is being enhanced, challenged, and in some cases, redefined.

Data is no longer just a tool for analysis; it has become an active participant in the creative process. In fields like music, art, literature, and design, AI-powered systems are generating original works, composing symphonies, creating paintings, and even writing poetry. Algorithms trained on vast datasets can identify patterns in human creativity, predict trends, and produce content that rival's human-generated work. Platforms like OpenAI's DALL·E, DeepMind's AlphaFold, and generative music tools showcase how machines can contribute to artistic and scientific breakthroughs.

Beyond the arts, data is driving innovation in industries such as product design, marketing, and engineering. Companies leverage big data to analyze consumer behavior, predict market trends, and design products that better meet user needs. In architecture and urban planning, AI-driven simulations enable designers to optimize spaces for functionality, sustainability, and aesthetics — reshaping the way cities evolve.

However, this data-driven shift raises important questions: Where does human creativity end and machine creativity begin? Can an algorithm truly "innovate," or is it merely recombining existing knowledge? While AI can generate ideas, it lacks the emotional depth, cultural context, and subjective experience that define human creativity. The most groundbreaking innovations will likely emerge from the synergy between human intuition and machine intelligence — where data serves as a catalyst rather than a replacement.

The future of creativity and innovation will belong to those who embrace data as a collaborator. Professionals who understand how to work alongside AI, interpret its outputs, and infuse human insights into the creative process will thrive. Whether in business, technology, or the arts, the next great wave of innovation will be shaped by those who master the balance between data-driven efficiency and human originality.

The Social Impact of AI-Driven Decision-Making

As artificial intelligence becomes more embedded in everyday life, its role in decision-making is growing at an unprecedented pace. AI-driven algorithms now influence who gets a job interview, who is approved for a loan, what medical treatments are recommended, and even who is granted bail in the criminal justice system. These automated decisions, powered by vast amounts of data, offer efficiency and scalability that human judgment alone cannot match. However, they also raise profound social and ethical questions about fairness, accountability, and the unintended consequences of relying on machines to make critical choices.

The Benefits: Speed, Efficiency, and Objectivity

One of the key advantages of AI in decision-making is its ability to process enormous datasets rapidly, identifying patterns that may be invisible to human analysts. In healthcare, for instance, AI-powered diagnostic tools can detect early signs of disease with greater accuracy than traditional methods, potentially saving lives. In finance, AI models can assess credit risk based on non-traditional indicators, expanding access to loans for underserved populations. Businesses leverage AI to streamline hiring, reducing human bias by focusing on skill-based assessments rather than subjective impressions.

The Risks: Bias, Transparency, and Accountability

Despite its potential, AI-driven decision-making is far from neutral. Algorithms are only as good as the data they are trained on, and if that data reflects historical biases, AI can perpetuate or even amplify them. For example, hiring algorithms trained on past recruitment data may favor male candidates if historical hiring practices were biased against women. Predictive policing systems, designed to allocate law enforcement resources, have been criticized for disproportionately targeting minority communities, reinforcing existing societal inequalities.

A major challenge is the "black box" nature of many AI models. Unlike human decision-makers who can explain their reasoning, complex AI algorithms often operate in ways that are difficult to interpret, making it hard to challenge or audit their decisions. This lack of transparency can erode public trust, particularly in high-stakes areas such as healthcare, finance, and criminal justice.

Striking a Balance: Ethical AI for a Just Society

To mitigate these risks, organizations must adopt responsible AI practices. This includes ensuring algorithmic transparency, regularly auditing AI systems for bias, and incorporating human oversight into critical decision-making processes. Ethical AI frameworks, such as explainable AI (XAI) and fairness-aware machine learning, are emerging as essential tools for making AI decisions more understandable and accountable.

Furthermore, governments and regulatory bodies are stepping in to enforce fairness in AI applications. The European Union's AI Act, for instance, seeks to classify and regulate AI systems based on their level of risk, ensuring that high-risk applications undergo strict scrutiny. Such measures signal a growing recognition that AI-driven decision-making must align with societal values and human rights.

The Future of AI-Driven Decision-Making

As AI continues to evolve, its influence on social structures will only deepen. Striking the right balance between efficiency and fairness, automation and human oversight, innovation and ethical responsibility will be critical in shaping a future where AI-driven decisions benefit society as a whole. The age of data is not just about what machines can do—it is about how humanity chooses to wield this power.

Preparing for the Unknown: The Ethics and Governance of Future Technologies

As data-driven technologies advance at an unprecedented pace, society faces an urgent need to establish ethical frameworks and governance structures to manage their impact. Artificial intelligence, automation, and data analytics are reshaping industries, economies, and even human behavior in ways that are difficult to predict. While these technologies promise innovation and efficiency, they also introduce complex risks, from bias in AI decision-making to surveillance concerns and economic displacement. Preparing for the unknown requires a proactive approach to ethics, regulation, and governance to ensure that technological progress aligns with human values and societal well-being.

The Ethical Dilemmas of Emerging Technologies

The integration of AI, machine learning, and automation into critical systems, healthcare, finance, law enforcement, and governance—raises profound ethical questions. Key concerns include:

- Bias and Fairness – AI models trained on biased data can reinforce social inequalities, leading to unfair hiring practices, discriminatory lending decisions, and biased policing.

- Privacy and Surveillance – As data collection becomes more pervasive, individuals risk losing control over their personal information. Governments and corporations must strike a balance between security and individual rights.

- Accountability and Transparency – Many AI systems operate as "black boxes," making it difficult to understand or challenge decisions made by algorithms. Ensuring transparency is crucial for trust.

- Autonomy vs. Control – The increasing role of AI in decision-making prompts debates about human oversight. Should autonomous systems have the final say in medical diagnoses, criminal sentencing, or financial approvals?

As we navigate these dilemmas, ethical considerations must be embedded in the design, deployment, and governance of new technologies.

Regulatory Challenges in a Rapidly Evolving Landscape

Technology is evolving faster than regulatory frameworks can adapt. Many governments struggle to craft policies that protect consumers and businesses without stifling innovation. Some key governance challenges include:

- Global vs. Local Regulation – With data and AI systems operating across borders, different countries have conflicting regulatory approaches. The EU's GDPR focuses on privacy, while China emphasizes state oversight. How can global standards be established?

- Balancing Innovation with Control – Overregulation could slow down technological progress, while under-regulation could lead to uncontrolled risks, such as the misuse of AI in warfare or deepfake-driven misinformation campaigns.

- Corporate Responsibility vs. Government Oversight – Should tech giants self-regulate, or should governments impose stricter controls? History has shown that self-regulation often falls short in protecting public interests.

The challenge lies in designing policies that anticipate future risks while remaining flexible enough to adapt to new developments.

Governance Models for Future Technologies

To create a more ethical and sustainable technological future, organizations and governments are exploring different governance models:

- Ethical AI Guidelines; organizations like the IEEE and OECD have proposed ethical frameworks for AI development, emphasizing fairness, transparency, and accountability.

- Public-Private Partnerships – Governments and technology firms are increasingly collaborating to establish best practices, such as AI ethics boards and independent oversight committees.

- Decentralized Governance Models – With the rise of blockchain and decentralized systems, new governance models are emerging that distribute decision-making power rather than concentrating it in a few hands.

These governance models will shape how society navigates the uncertainties of the digital age.

Future-Proofing Society Against Unforeseen Technological Risks

While it is impossible to predict every technological breakthrough or societal disruption, there are steps we can take to prepare for the unknown:

- Investing in Digital Literacy and Education – Equipping individuals with the skills to understand and critically engage with technology is essential for an informed society.

- Implementing Ethical AI Practices from the Ground Up – Developers and businesses should prioritize fairness, inclusivity, and accountability in AI system design.

- Encouraging Global Cooperation – Cross-border collaboration on ethical and legal standards will help prevent misuse and create a more unified approach to governance.

- Creating Adaptive Regulatory Frameworks – Policymakers must embrace agile governance models that evolve alongside technological advancements.

The Age of Data is redefining humanity, and with it comes the responsibility to shape a future where technology serves society, rather than the other way around. By addressing ethics and governance proactively, we can harness the benefits of data-driven innovation while mitigating its risks.

www.ingramcontent.com/pod-product-compliance
Lightning Source LLC
LaVergne TN
LVHW092007090526
838202LV00001B/41